New Jersey Mob

Memoirs of a Top Cop

by

Bob Buccino

DORRANCE
PUBLISHING CO
EST. 1920
PITTSBURGH, PENNSYLVANIA 15238

Dorrance Publishing Co
585 Alpha Drive
Pittsburgh, PA 15238
Visit our website at www.dorrancebookstore.com

ISBN: 978-1-4809-2378-2
eISBN: 978-1-4809-2907-4

YOU WILL NOT FIND ANY REFERENCES OR FOOTNOTES IN THIS BOOK.

THE BOOK IS COMPLETELY MY MEMOIR. EVERY EVENT IN THE BOOK IS FROM MY DIRECT KNOWLEDGE AND MEMORIES.

SINCE IT'S FROM MY RECOLLECTION, THERE MAY BE SOME ERRORS, BUT I WAS CAREFUL TO BE AS ACCURATE AS POSSIBLE.

I DIDN'T WANT TO MAKE IT A TYPICAL POLICE BOOK, SO I SELECTED THE CASES THAT I FELT WOULD BE OF INTEREST TO THE READER.

THE BOOK IS IN THREE PARTS:

PART ONE – GROWING UP WITH THE MAFIA. GETTING MY EDUCATION IN ORGANIZED CRIME. BEING A WANNABE AND RUNNING MY OWN BOOKMAKING AND SHAKEDOWN OPERATIONS.

PART TWO – I BECOME A STATE TROOPER. IN 1957 DRUGS HIT STREETS AND I GOT MARRIED. IT CHANGED MY LIFE. I BECAME A TROOPER.

PART THREE – MY ENCOUNTERS WITH THE COSA NOSTRA. SOME OF MY INTERESTING CASES.

YOU WILL FIND WHEN READING THIS BOOK THAT IN MANY CASES I USE INITIALS OR FICTITIOUS NAMES. THERE WEREN'T ANY LEGAL REASONS. I CERTAINLY COULD HAVE. I DID IT FOR SEVERAL REASONS. MANY INDIVIDUALS DID THEIR TIME, AND THERE WASN'T GOOD REASON TO REHASH THEIR PASTS IN RESPECT TO THEIR FAMILIES. LAW ENFORCEMENT OFFICERS WERE MENTIONED IN A HUMOROUS WAY. I CERTAINLY DIDN'T WANT TO EMBARRASS THEM.

I HOPE YOU ENJOY THE BOOK.

Contents

Prologue 1

My career in the state police, State Commission of Investigation, the Division
of Criminal Justice, and the Union County Prosecutor's Office has been very
rewarding. I have satisfied my goal to significantly reduce the existence of
the Cosa Nostra in New Jersey. I didn't do it alone. I had outstanding support. The New Jersey state police, an outstanding, top-of-the-line law enforcement agency, provided quality troopers and leadership to our mission.
Without that organization I would never have developed my expertise. I
would be remiss if I didn't mention the Alcohol, Tax, and Firearm Agency
for their excellent assistance and expertise. The FBI provided intelligence and
cooperation in furtherance to our mission. Local police departments provided a great deal of lead information and manpower without which we
would have never reached our goal.

During my tenure, my task forces arrested and successfully prosecuted
four Bosses, one consigliere, one Underboss, five capodecimo, seventy-two
soldiers, and two hundred and twenty seven street-level associates (bookmakers, loan sharks, and narcotic traffickers.) There were over 300 significant investigations that were conducted during this time period. The stats
used were up to the year 1986. There were other cases that I have not included because my book would go through the roof. Following, I have listed
some of the most significant cases.

Tiger Management – The Lucchese crime family under Capo Peter Chioda
started a transportation brokerage company in Port Newark, New Jersey.
They were attempting the transportation of garbage generated in New York

and New Jersey to out-of-state landfills. Seven members of the Lucchese family were indicted for a homicide related to this case.

Operation Purdue – Fraudulent obtaining of several million dollars in public construction contracts. Arrested and convicted Genovese soldier Frank "Chickee" Muscato.

Operation Leaf – Combined three separate investigations into the criminal activities that included murder and distribution of narcotics by the Bruno, Colombo, Lucchese, and Bonnano crime families. Fifty-five individuals were arrested and convicted.

Operation North – Daniel Provensano, the nephew of the notorious Capo Anthony "Tony Pro" Provensano, committed a series of extortions in an attempt to take over an insurance company by kidnapping and terrorizing the victim and his family. Prosecuted and convicted.

Operation Point Pleasant – Five members of the Colombo crime family having a meeting in reference to their internal war in New York. They were arrested and turned over to New York authorities.

I have to recognize the outstanding detectives and attorneys who worked with me; without them this book would never have been produced. Ron Donahue, Paul Smith, Jim Sweeney, Mike McGaughran, Dennis Masucci, Bobby Jones, Charlie Kyle, Jim Russo, Vince Gagliardi, Kenney Hogan, Tommy Adams, Ritchy Adams, Joe Falcone, Bob Carroll, John Matthews, Bob Winters, Bob Codey, Bill Newsome, Nick Oriolo, Kevin Foley, Sal Apuzzio, Brian McCarthy, Jack Elko, John Cerefice, Steve LaPenta Dom Polifron, Anthony Bruno, and I am certain I am forgetting several persons. My apology.

PHOTO - ME AND DONALD TRUMP

PHOTO - HAVING A GOOD LAUGH WITH DONALD TRUMP

Prologue 2

I have been in law enforcement for over fifty-one years. I grew up in Orange, New Jersey, where there was a large Italian community. When I was growing up, I not only hung out with members of the Cosa Nostra (organized crime family), but I wanted to be one of them

This all changed in 1957 when I got married. At this time, I was witnessing a transition in my neighborhood that would forever change its landscape. Heroin was being brought in and pushed by the Sicilian Mafia and being sold everywhere. I had to break away from my old gang and become a hardworking stiff to support my family.

Now with heroin on the streets, the thought of living life as a mobster didn't seem so glamorous. Besides, my wife would have nothing to do with me if that was the direction I wanted to take. It appeared to be the only option at the time for me and most of the boys I grew up with like Anthony Accetturo. So, I figured if you can't join them, beat them.

I started my career as a New Jersey state trooper in 1962. At the same time, Anthony started his career as a member of the Cosa Nostra. As it turns out, our careers would not only start, but end at the same time. As a matter of fact, our careers had many parallels. When Anthony rose in the Cosa Nostra, I rose in rank within the NJ state police.

I was very successful throughout my years with the NJ state police and later as the deputy chief in charge of the Statewide Organized Crime and Racketeering Task Force for the New Jersey attorney general's office. Through the efforts of my task force, the seven Cosa Nostra families operating in New Jersey were eventually dismantled. In fact, over 475 members

of the Cosa Nostra families operating in New Jersey were arrested, indicted, and convicted during my tenure.

Along the way, there were many "behind the scenes" stories. Some were heartbreaking, and some were quite humorous. I used to tell my family and friends some of the stories, and I became inspired to write this book at their numerous suggestions. Each of my attempts to do so over the years always came to a grinding halt for one reason or another. I knew I wanted to put my stories to paper, but I also knew I didn't want it to be another cop's book. I wanted to tell my whole story from the beginning so that not only would one enjoy reading it, but it also might make a good movie, because my story plays out just like a movie would. There are amusing and interesting encounters that you will read about as I take you through my career from a uniformed trooper to detective to commander of organized crime cases.

The Cosa Nostra has been a part of my entire life. When I was a young boy, I knew of the existence of the good fellas, and in over forty years of investigating the Cosa Nostra, I have earned the right to say that no one, and I mean no one, knows the New Jersey Mob like I do.

My maternal grandparents arrived in the United States from Palermo, Sicily around the year 1900. My grandfather was an aristocrat. His family owned land back in Sicily, having a church as well as a college on their property. My grandmother, Antonina Nicosia, was a peasant woman who was attending their college when she and my grandfather fell in love. Since they were not of the same social standard, they left Sicily to marry and start a life in America. They first lived in Brooklyn, where my grandmother continued her education and became a midwife. My grandfather never worked a day in his life. He was always dressed like a Don in tailored shirts, suits, etc. My grandmother supported the family. They moved to Orange, New Jersey, where my grandmother prospered and was highly respected. She bought a home, was the first woman in Orange to drive a car, and was the first to have a telephone in their home. They had four children: two boys and two girls. Every other week, my grandmother and her lady friends would go to Brooklyn to visit family and buy their Italian food products. In the early '20s there was this thing called the Black Hand, which was a group of Italian thugs that extorted from Italian businessmen and women. If one resisted, their business or home would be bombed or torched.

The Sicilians feared the Black Hand. My grandmother became the recipient of Black Hand messages, which were pieces of paper with a drawing or an ink print of a black hand. This was the initial act that would impose the fear that would result in the victim complying with the extortion demands. My grandmother was scared to death, and on one trip to Brooklyn she told one of her lady friends of the dilemma. Her friend suggested they stop over her cousin's apartment and see if he could help. My grandmother took her suggestion. My mother recalled the cousin as being an ugly man who sat at the kitchen table eating spaghetti as my grandmother showed him the Black Hand paper and asked for his help. He told my grandmother that she was a good, hard-working Sicilian woman, and did not have to worry about the Black Hand. He told her that someone would pay her a visit and would become her contact person if she received any more threats. My grandmother told him how grateful she was and kissed his cheeks. Before they left the ugly man's apartment, he called my grandmother to the side and told her that he was behind on his rent and owed money. He asked if she could lend him some money, which she did without hesitation. My mother didn't know the amount, but she knew it was a lot, considering the times. A man did come to visit my grandmother in Orange and assured her that she wouldn't have any more problems with the Black Hand—and she didn't. Several months went by and her friend's cousin still didn't repay the loan, so my grandmother stopped by his apartment to ask for repayment of the loan. When she did, he responded in Sicilian, "You asked me once, don't ever ask me twice." It was then that my grandmother realized she had been extorted. This ugly man's name was Vito Genovese, who later became the Boss of the Cosa Nostra family that still bears his name. After this favor, and because my grandmother accepted the protection of Vito Genovese, she was then forced to perform abortions for associates of the Genovese family when they knocked up their girlfriends. My grandmother died in her forties of a massive stroke. After her death, my grandfather left his children and went back to Sicily. My mother, Josephine, raised her three siblings along with my Aunt Mamie, my grandmother's sister.

This kind of extortion has never changed and has been the bread and butter for the Mafia through the years. They set up a scenario that will create fear in their proposed victim. The victim goes to a "friend" for help, not knowing that it was the friend who created the scenario in the first place. After the friend "takes care of the problem," the extortion begins. They usually start small, like asking for a small loan. Then they will ask if the victim could hire a friend, a no-show job for an associate, eventually infiltrating the business to the point of a takeover.

Italian immigrants built this country of ours, first with their hands, then with their brains and determination. I am very proud of my heritage. Italian-American gangsters represent one-hundredth of one percent of the Italian-Americans in this country, yet many hard working Italian-Americans, especially in the construction industry, carry the stigma of the mob. There is a saying that when an Italian immigrant only has a wheelbarrow and a shovel to make a living, he is called a guinea or a wop. After he works hard and saves some money, begins to prosper and buys a dump truck, he is called the Mafia. These criminals have been glamorized by television and the movies but are in fact a cancer to all Italian-Americans. We can eliminate this cancer. My grandmother fell victim to these so-called "Men of Honor Mafioso." Fifty years later, her grandson would revenge the Mafia's extortion of Antonina Nicolina. That grandson was me.

Chapter One

The Gravy Pot

I was born on Hurlburt Street in Orange on March 26, 1938. The City of Orange is located about three miles from the City of Newark. Its population varied from twenty-eight thousand to thirty-five thousand. Italian Americans comprised the largest ethnic group, which hovered at fifty percent. The rest of the city consisted of about thirty percent black, and the remaining twenty percent were Irish and German. The city, small in size, about a one square mile, had segregated YMCAs. The Italian one was located on Hurlburt Street in the center of the Italian community. The black one was on Oakwood Avenue in the center of the black community, a large YMCA on Main Street on the East Orange/Orange line, and a YWCA also on Main Street.

My parents bought a house on Scotland Road, and that is where my brother, three sisters, and I grew up. My cousins all grew up in apartments, and since my parents owned a home, all the cousins would visit our house on Sundays. My mother made enough gravy (tomato sauce) to feed an army, and as each relative would arrive, they would go right to the pot cooking on the stove and steal a meatball or a piece of sausage, or perhaps just dip a piece of bread in the gravy and eat it. My father would remind them "not to eat his braciole." Every Sunday was a like a festival in my house. The day would begin with my mother waking us up early because we had to make the nine o'clock mass at Mt. Carmel Church, which was about a mile walk. Sundays were so special then. I fondly remember the smell of sausage frying and gravy simmering, and the lazy sounds of the family awakening. Mom

1

never could make crispy bacon. I guess Italian mothers don't like to make anything without garlic or gravy. She would make Italian-style eggs, better known as moonstruck eggs. You know, a slice of toasted round Italian bread with a hole cut out with a fried egg in the center, or perhaps an egg or two poached in the gravy.

My parents were so old school that if I looked pale, instead of medicine, my father would give me a raw egg in a little muscatel or sherry wine to gulp down. You remember that scene in Rocky when he cracked open a bunch of eggs and drank them? Yeah, that kind of medicine. Sometimes, it would be just an egg with a small hole in it, and I would have to eat it by sucking it out of the shell (hence the phrase "go suck an egg"). The home remedies didn't stop there. If it was deemed that any of us kids looked "sick," out would come the Farina. We would all have to eat it to keep from catching anything from each other. The deal was to eat fast and try to beat my siblings, Rose, Nicky, Nina, and Pat, to the one and only bathroom. I don't know why, but I still dream of that bathroom. Maybe it was the foreboding presence of the dreaded enema bag that always hung on the bathroom door and was always ready for use with the first sign of any, and I mean *any*, pain or discomfort. Having three sisters made it nearly impossible for me to get in that bathroom.

Mom would give me three nickels for the three collections during mass at Mt. Carmel Church, with the final instructions each week, "Don't forget to stop and see Aunt Mamie, Aunt Sadie, Uncle Cheech, Aunt Columbia, Cousin Josey, Cousin Gertrude, AND DON'T FORGET TO PICK UP THE BREAD." I was fully schooled on how to pick the bread out from the bakers. You have to squeeze it, or, as my mother would add, "they will sell you yesterday's bread." I was a good kid and I didn't ever want to disappoint my mother when it came to getting the right bread. But of course, by the time I got the bread home, it no longer had heels.

Along the way home I would meet up with my gang of friends: Red, Toochie, Jimmy Boy, Moon Mullins, and Frankie. We would walk through the Italian section of town smelling the wonderful aromas of garlic meats frying and gravies simmering. "Look, its wine-making season," someone would yell out. That meant that crates upon crates of grapes would line the sidewalks on Essex Avenue. Soon, every kid in the neighborhood would be riding a scooter made of a grape crate nailed to a piece of two-by-four with a roller skate attached to the front and rear of the wooden rail. Although very popular, getting the crates was not an easy task, and eating the grapes was even harder. The old men would yell, "Don't touch the grapes," at us kids. There were rumors of black widow spiders in the crates, and we were warned that "one bite and we would die." So getting crates took some courage. To this day, I'm still uneasy when I reach for a grape. I wonder if there were really black widow spiders or if that is what we were told so fear would make sure we didn't pick at the grapes.

In church, we were little angels; sort of. After church, I would have two nickels left from the three mom gave me for the collections at church, so I could play the pinball machines at Louie the Horse's luncheonette. Although it was never my fault, sometimes I would miss mass and *have* to go to Louie's instead. When that would happen, I would have to find a church flyer to bring home as proof that I attended mass.

Walking down Essex Avenue, all at once those familiar aromas engage my interest. Pork, meatballs, sausage and braciole frying, and garlic laden gravies simmering created an intoxicating aroma that filled the air. The fragrance of Italian cooking was wondrous. My Aunt Mamie always had a beautiful tomato and basil garden, and the Italian bakery would be just bringing out the hot Italian rolls. I can still taste that tomato crushed in the hot bread with a little olive oil and oregano from my Aunt's window sill—left especially for me. After paying respect to my relatives (playing the pinball machines at the Horse's), I would always be running late. I had to be home by noon with the bread, the bread without heels that would be keeping the tomato in my stomach company.

When I arrived home, my house was already filled with relatives. Freddy Bell, Mikey, Anthony, Dante, Little Joey, the Canduras, Big Joey, the Menzas and Uncle Joe. Good 'ol Uncle Joe. He would give me a quarter to find my father's good wine and bring him a glassful of it. My father would be sitting at the kitchen table with a gallon of Barberone, surrounded by bottles of Anisette, Strega, and Grappa. I hardly remember my father wearing pants in the house. When he was home, he wore boxers in his house and didn't care if the president of the United States was coming over. Mom would make her famous gravy (not to be confused with sauce). Sunday was pork gravy, and what a gravy it was. Meatballs, sausage, pork stuffed with garlic, neck bones, pork skin, bracioli. Sometimes I imagine I can still hear the sizzling sound of tomatoes as mom dropped them into the hot olive oil in the old gravy pot. Mom had a gravy pot, and ONLY gravy was made in it. It was considered a sacrilege to put anything else in that pot. Uncle Eddy would also stop by. He was my mother's brother, and he would always bring with him some dandelions, gardoons, or mushrooms that he had picked on the way to our house. I liked Uncle Eddy. He too would give me a quarter to find my father's booze and pour him a water glass full of Four Roses whiskey. We kids would all be in the living room watching our new invention, an eight-inch Dumont television. Sunday was a bad day for television and kids. No Spy King, Commander Codey, Secret Squadron, or Roy Rodgers. All we could do was make fun of the kid talent shows and what dorks they were. Then mom would call out, "Mangia, mangia, it's time to eat." We would always eat with the pope at one thirty. Scafatones, gravy meat, a side of ricotta, insalada, and whatever was left of the bread. After we devoured the pasta, out would come the chicken, roasted with rosemary, garlic, and olive oil, and the potatoes. Oh, those potatoes were so good.

When dinner was over, we would finish up with espresso, anisette, biscotti, or my mother's ricotta pie. Soon the sound of a kitchen full of women chatting and washing dishes along with the sound of men snoring could be heard throughout the house. Later that night, whoever was left in the house would snack on the leftovers. Leftovers were just an overflow of food that my mom knew was going to be consumed by us later that night. When we ate again, it was like we never ate at all that day. Where did we put all of that food? The love, affection, and mutual family respect we shared during those days are un-equalled by today's modern family. As my own kids grew up, I tried to share this feeling with my children, but it was not the same. I suppose it has to do with neighborhoods being what they were. Most of my family has moved out of the traditional Italian community that we grew up in, including me. We all have families now, and we only get together at weddings and funerals. Everyone has passed on. Mom and dad died years apart. Dad died before mom, but we buried mom's heart when we buried him. She never showed sadness to us, but we could tell. Sundays were never the same. Despite the passing of time, the magic of Sunday still lives on in my memory. These memories inspire me to make gravy every Sunday, and I remember whether I'm alone or with my family. I always use the same pot to make the gravy, the same pot my mother used. In doing so, I pay tribute to the past and keep alive the traditions I so deeply adore. By keeping the tradition of Sunday, I honor the memory of my mother and my father. Now when the meal is over and all is calm, I drink a glass of Barberone. As I do this, I can picture my father at the kitchen table in his boxers, and in my heart of hearts, during the magic moment when I drop the tomatoes into the pot of hot olive oil, I can hear my mother's voice, "Mangia, mangia, it's time to eat."

Chapter Two

The Orange Mafia

Along with the Irish and Jewish mobs, the American Mafia made an enormous amount of money during the Prohibition Era. During the late '20s and early '30s, they ran speakeasies, horse parlors, gambling halls, and produced and imported booze from Canada and other countries. The Italian mob controlled the trucking of the booze. When Prohibition was repealed in 1933, the mob had to find another way to make this kind of money. They decided to take control of the numbers racket and the trucking union (which later became the Teamsters). Furthermore, the assassination of the two mafia Bosses Guiseppe Massera and Salvatore Marranzano, orchestrated by Lucky Lucania (Luciano), produced a new set of American Mafia families, which now consisted of seven in total. Five of these families were in New York, one was in New Jersey, and one in Philadelphia.

As a kid growing up in Orange, New Jersey, I saw the wise guys and recognized the Mafia long before the FBI even acknowledged their existence. The numbers racket was prevalent. Everybody played their favorite number and knew the numbers man. You could place a horse bet or place a wager on almost any sport contest in almost every candy store and luncheonette. I would see the wise guys in front of their social club or tavern openly doing their business of exchanging money or betting slips. Yes, we would also see the patrolmen frolicking with the wise guys. Everyone knew someone who took a beating or mysteriously disappeared for failing to pay money owed to a bookmaker.

Every Thursday was collection day, and the bookmakers and loan sharks would be at the White Castle on the corner of Scotland Road and Central Avenue. Every Monday during football season, the football tickets for the week were handed out. This would become very

lucrative for me. By the time I made it to high school, I was earning over one hundred dollars a week as a controller. So were most of my friends. We also knew the "made" guys in the neighborhood. Red Cecere, Gyp De-Carlo, and the Boot Bioardo were men of "respect." When there was a wake for an Italian from the neighborhood, the made guys would make it a point to be seen giving an envelope to the widow of the deceased. We kids would hang out at a candy store or luncheonette playing the pinball machines that we knew were owned by the mob's "Runyon Sales." Of course, these machines paid off in money, not game credits.

When one of the wise guys would visit the establishment while we were playing the pinball machines, he would throw a handful of nickels on the machine for us to play. We admired these guys. To this day, I believe we were being trained to be the future wise guys or degenerate gamblers. There were blackjack and monte games held in the basement of our church. We would have the nickel and dime games, and the adults would be playing for serious money. I can still see Little Pussy Russo in his pink Cadillac in front of the drug store in West Orange. Boy did I have a vision to be just like him someday.

The holidays were gratuity days for the police. We would see the officers as they received their envelopes in open view and in broad daylight. Many of the officers would salute the wise guys as they received their gift.

Outside of the gambling, we were good kids. Except for the booze, there weren't any drugs around in those days. As a kid, the worst thing we would do was steal some of our father's homemade wine and cigarettes and smoke and drink.

Chapter Three

Teenage Years

During the late forties and early fifties, no one gave a second thought about gambling being illegal or wrong in any way. It was a way of life; *the* way of life. After all we had card games in the basement of the church. All we did was play sports. In those days, the playgrounds and the Ys were always full of kids playing sports. The Italian Y always had a boxing ring up, and we all learned the art of fighting. Tony Galento, who was famous for his knock-down of Joe Louis, would stand on the top step of the Y and play King of the Hill with us. We had to try to pass him as he guarded the entrance to the Y by throwing us down the stairs. I was friends with his son, Tony, Jr. who was my age. Funny thing about Tony Jr., he looked exactly like his father. Scar tissue and pug looking. Only thing wrong with this picture is that Jr. never had a fight in his life and was a pussycat. When we weren't playing sports, we would be smoking cigarettes and drinking our father's homemade wine that one of us swiped. Back then it was cool to smoke cigarettes. Our hairstyles were cool too. We all wore what was called the Chicago Box. Square back, flat top, and long sides with the back combed into a duck ass. Royal blue or rust jackets and pants. Pistol pockets and pegged pants with saddle stitching were the in style. Shoes were important too, but they had to have a square toe or forget about it. If we were just hanging out, blue jeans and a white T-shirt with the sleeve rolled up with a pack of cigarettes inside was the only attire considered cool. The Fonzie character from *Happy Days* would have been considered a "fag" in our neighborhood.

At night, we would be on the corner of Scotland Road and Franklin Street singing and trying to imitate the Four Aces, The Ink Spots, the Four Lads, or Frankie Lane. There weren't pizzerias on every corner in those days, but the Star Tavern and the Toast of the Town made pies you would die for. There weren't any sub or hoagie places either like there is now. We would go into an Italian deli and grab a ten-cent sandwich which consisted of a loaf of crusty Italian bread that would be stuffed with the ends of the cold cuts. Prosciutto, salami, mortadello, imported provolone or sometimes ricotta, roasted peppers, crushed Italian olives, and a sprinkle of olive oil. Forget the lettuce and mayonnaise. I didn't even know what mayonnaise was until I was in my twenties.

Around middle school age, we had our own club, "The Crusaders." We bought jackets and even had a handmade clubhouse in the lots behind my house. We did everything together, but mostly played sports. In order to become a member of the Crusaders, one had to take a loyalty test, which consisted of pricking of fingers and exchanging blood. We believed this would make us blood brothers. Actually, it was an oath similar to the Mafia's. I don't know why or how we started doing that. The Crusaders mainly consisted of me, Red (today a millionaire and successful businessman with RJ Reynolds), Tooch (a barber), Frankie I (president of shipping of a large oil company), Ralphie (deceased) Frankie R., Scootch, Bobby Gray (the Nazi), Moon Mullins, and Rocco Accetturo, who was a good kid, but tough. However, his younger brother by one year, Anthony Accetturo, was a trouble maker. He was tough as nails and always appeared as if he was just in a fight. I used to kick him in the ass and chase him. One day he broke into the clubhouse, removed his shoes, and took a nap. When we arrived we could smell his feet. They smelled like provolone cheese. It was disgusting. I gave him the nickname of "Dirty Feet." I thought it was the best nickname ever, but he didn't like that. I stopped calling him that when he got hooked up with the wise guys in East Orange. Anthony later became the Boss of New Jersey's Lucchese crime family.

PHOTO - DO I LOOK LIKE A MOB GUY?

Chapter Four

Wannabe

I was a good student until I went to high school. My parents had saved enough money to send me to either Seton Hall Prep, Newark Academy, or St. Benedict's, but I protested something terrible to the idea of being sent to a "fag" school. I just would not go. They gave up and I went to Orange High. Boy, what a mistake. My friends who went to one of the prep schools all became either attorneys or doctors. I always remembered my parents' failed attempt to send me to prep school and swore that someday I would send a son to prep school and he would not have any say in the matter. I was fortunate to send my youngest son, Rob, to Blair Academy, and today he is a biochemical engineer. I am very proud of him. Anyway, my education stopped the day I stepped foot in Orange High. Actually, it was regarded as an excellent high school, and many students went on to college and became very successful. I became a wise guy. I broke away from my friends and the Crusaders and considered the older guys as my friends. I never did homework and did just enough to pass my classes. Every night I would hang out at Schimele's Pool Hall, the White Castle, or the Busy Bee (an Italian hot dog store). I think I ate an Italian hot dog or White Castle every day of my life until I got married. I thought my complexion was naturally a shade of green until I changed my diet.

Gambling was the way of life, and I did my share. I started running numbers, selling football pools, and ran small nickel and dime card games and everything else that was around in those days. I always had money in my pocket. I idealized the wise guys like Little Pussy Russo in his pink Cadillac convertible in the neighborhood, watching Red Cecere receiving respect from everyone who passed him on the street. I admired that way of life and wanted to be a wise guy. No one messed with the made guys in the neighborhood. At the same time that I was playing the role of a smalltime wannabe, Anthony Accetturo was starting to make a name for himself in the Vailsburg Section of Newark.

I was hanging out with older guys and right alongside the local wise guys. The wise guys used to hang out and conduct their business either at the White Castle or the Beverly Lounge on Essex Avenue. I was becoming part of them. I would observe the loan sharks at the White Castle making collections and threatening guys for missing a payment. I would see and admire Little Pussy Russo in his pink Cadillac convertible driving through Orange and going to Lombard's Pharmacy on Main Street in West Orange. At night, I would hang out at Schimele's Pool Hall. All the wannabees would be there. I liked to fight in those days, and had quite a few. I quit sports and had my own bookmaking operation. I loved football season because I moved a lot of football tickets. I was making over one hundred dollars a week. I began shaking down students for, believe it or not, ten cents a week. There was a big black kid who I will call James who I got along with. I was collecting a dime a week from him, but one day when I asked him for the dime, he said, "Buccino, I ain't giving you no more dimes." He was eating an ice cream cone at the time and I pulled a James Cagney act and shoved the ice cream into his face. He responded by throwing a hay maker punch and knocked me on my ass. From the floor I said, "James, you don't have to pay me no more." This incident must have had some influence on me when I decided not to be a wise guy. I was making a lot of money as a seventeen year old. My girlfriend, Priscilla, who later became my wife, was the prettiest girl in school. In the fifties, one of the best Italian restaurants in Orange was Luigi's on Forest Street. Every Friday I had a table reserved for Pris and me, and we would be treated royally. Boy I loved that life.

I also had big balls. I had a motor vehicle incident with one of the old guys who was an associate of the Genovese family. He cut me off, so I chased him right to the Genovese club on

Day Street. There was a group of wise guys in front and he drove up front, got out, and went into the club. I drove up the sidewalk, ran into the club, and kicked the shit out of him. The Boss of the club, Toughie Zuppo, lived across the street in a second floor apartment that had a balcony over-looking the club. His Pisanos from the club started calling him, and when he came to the balcony they told him that the Buccino kid had beaten Muchie up. I came out of the club, my face sweaty and red, and Toughie yelled over to me, "How old are you?" I said, "Seventeen, why?" He responded, "Go back in and kick his ass again!" I knew I had made good with Toughy, be-cause after that incident, I had begun to receive respect in the neighborhood. Another time, we were going to a party and there were a half a dozen wannabees standing in front of the house. Pris was walking in front of me when one of the guys walked toward her and said, "Priscilla, baby," and that was the last word out of his mouth, because I broke his nose. It was a serious punch, because he was hospitalized for several days. When he got out I heard a rumor that he was going to get even with me. I waited until I saw him at the White Castle with several of his friends. I walked right in and went up to him and said, "Fish, I heard you were looking for me." He chick-ened right out and said, "There's no hard feelings. I'm sorry for saying some-thing stupid to Pris. I meant no harm." He extended his hand and we shook. This was one of the ways I started noticing respect from the neighborhood. Pris and I were dating for three years, and the relationship would be off and on during that time. When we weren't seeing each other, which was usually for a week or two at a time, Priscilla would go out with a guy named Charlie. He was a little older and had his own business and drove a new Caddy. Dur-ing one of our breakups, she called me to let me know that Charlie had bought an engagement ring, and she offered me an ultimatum. That was easy. We made up and she broke up with Charlie, but he was not giving up so easily. So one night I saw his Caddy parked by the side of the White Cas-tle. I had a forty-nine Pontiac and drove it right into the side of his Caddy. He came running out and saw his car and then looked over at me and backed off. I was a young mob guy in the making.

I became close friends with Billy Smuggler, Anthony Yacovino, and Doc. Billy and Yac later died of heroin overdoses. But in the early fifties and when I was with them, there weren't any drugs on the street. I never even saw a marijuana cigarette. Yac was one of the toughest guys in Orange, and Billy Smuggler was just plain nuts. Smuggler would start the fights and Yac and I would have to finish them. I didn't know that Yac's parents came from the same town in Sicily as my grandparents until one day when I went to call for him. He lived upstairs from Seagoing Tom's tavern. His grandfather had just arrived from Sicily to spend his last days with his family. When I went into the apartment, Yac was in the bathroom getting ready when his mother introduced me to his grandfather who immediately fell to his knees and started kissing my hand. His mother spoke to him in Sicilian and told him who my grandfather was. The old man had worked his entire life for my great-grandfather and my grandfather, and by kissing my hand he was paying his respect to my family. I kind of liked the show of respect the old man gave me, but all I could think of at the time was Yac seeing this and kicking my ass, and he almost did. We wound up exchanging a couple of body shots and laughed about it later

Doc was a hardworking hustler doing whatever he had to in order to make a few bucks. When the fourth of July would come around, he would go to North Carolina and bring back fireworks and sell them from the trunk of his car. After I became a state trooper, he stopped by my house one early July Sunday blowing his horn to tell me that he just got pulled over for speeding by a state trooper, with his trunkload of freshly imported fireworks from his annual trip to North Carolina. When I went outside it took me a moment to recognize him because it had been a few years since I last saw him. He proceeded to tell me about being pulled over and told me that he mentioned my name to the Trooper who pulled him over. The Trooper told him that he would not give him a ticket, but that he would be expecting a phone call from me. Imagine Doc telling me that he had a load of illegal fireworks and that he expected me to call the Trooper to thank him for giving Doc a break. I could have arrested him on the spot, but I just didn't have the heart to do so. But anyway, that was Doc. I bet he is still selling fireworks from the trunk of his car.

Billy would do insurance fraud scams; I had enough sense in those days not to get involved. He would either have a couple thousand dollars on him, having just been paid off by an insurance company, or would be dead broke and borrowing from the shys. One of his scams was to go to a car dealership and ask to test ride a used car. He would cut one of the brake lines and pump out the brake fluid. He then would either follow a conspirator and ram the car, or drive into a brick wall. Of course he would need an ambulance and a couple days in the hospital and in a short time collect a couple of thousand from the dealership and the insurance company. One time, there was a vacant car parked in front of the White Castle that was struck by another car. Before the police arrived, there were four persons injured in the car, including Billy.

They didn't even know whose car it was, but they all collected. Billy was cut off by the shylocks and needed money. He asked me to borrow one hundred dollars from Zip for him. I never knew Zip's real name. He was short and of a small build and carried a knife. I borrowed the money and agreed to pay twenty-five dollars per week for five weeks. Every week I would ask Billy if he paid Zip, and of course he always said he did, until one day Zip approached me and asked for all the money. It was now over three-hundred dollars that was owed. When I told Zip it was for Billy, he told me he knew my father and would go see him for the money. I could never allow this to happen. I knew Billy had just collected on a scam because he had just bought a new Buick convertible. I went home, got an axe, and went over to Billy's house. I blew the horn until he came out. I held the axe over his head and made him sign the bill of sale for the Buick over to me. After a couple of days he told me he paid off Zip. After I confirmed it with Zip, I gave him back his bill of sale. A couple of months later, Billy was able to borrow money from Zip. Of course, he didn't pay him back and ignored Zip's threats. One day, Yac, Billy, and I were sitting in Billy's Buick behind the White Castle when Zip opened the car door with knife in hand. We bailed out the other side of the car, and Billy and I started running down Scotland Road being chased by Zip. Yac had gotten back in the car and drove in front of us. He got out of the car, opened the trunk, and threw the jack in the air as we approached him. This was the whole bumper jack, not just the handle. Billy caught the jack on the fly, turned, and swung the jack, hitting Zip right on the top of his head. Zip went to his knees bleeding like a pig. Billy, Yac, and I got into the car and locked the doors. I knew we were in serious trouble when Zip stood by the door shaking the car with his blood-covered face with knife still in hand. The old man never fell to the ground. The shot he took in the head definitely needed medical attention. We took off and stayed out of sight until Billy's brother, who was connected to Red Cecere, a made guy, had a sit down and saved his brother's life. Wherever we went, Billy would create an incident that would either end in a fight or us talking a police officer out of arresting us. One time, we decided to go see Count Basie at the Latin Quarters. We made our connection through one of the wise guys in Red Cecere's crew. When we mentioned the right name, we were treated royally. This happened a couple of times; not only at the Latin Quarters, but also at the Copacabana. While watching the Count (Basie, that is), don't you know a pickpocket tried to pick Billy's wallet. We were onto the guy because we saw him working the room. He made a very poor choice in picking Billy's wallet. Not only because Billy didn't have ten cents to his name, but because our guys would've had a big reaction to have been ripped off. We escorted him outside, took the wallets he had swiped from others away from him, and gave them to the bouncer who accompanied us, and Yac pounded the hell out of the pickpocket. I doubt that guy ever showed his face in the Latin Quarters again.

When we returned to New Jersey, Billy was all fired up. We stopped at a diner on South Orange Avenue in the Vailsburg Section of Newark. This was Campisi and Galicchio family territory. The Lucchese, Bonnanno, and Colombo families all had a piece of this area. Only the Bruno and Genovese guys didn't have much to do with the Vailsburg section of Newark. There was a small diner that was open all night. It was a place where all the local guys would go after the clubs closed for eggs and Italian sausage. The place was full, so we had to go to the furthest end and stand behind the last booth. There were two couples at the booth and they had two pitchers of beer. I was standing the closest to the booth when Billy leaned over and slapped one of the men on the back of the head. He did this in such a way that, when the guy turned around, he thought I did it. As this guy's eyes darted around trying to figure out who did it, he said, "Have a good laugh, but don't ever do it again." That was all Billy had to hear. Once the guy went back to his beer, Billy reached over and slapped the guy again. This time the guy stood up, smashed the two pitchers in his hands and put me against the wall with the jagged ends against my throat. I begged and cried like a baby. I thought my life was over. Billy triple talked the guy and he eventually calmed down. After a thousand apologies, the guy returned to his seat. I was pissed and wanted to kick Billy's ass. I wanted to leave, but both Billy and Yac calmed Rue down and convinced me to at least eat my eggs that were being served. As soon as we finished and were starting to leave, Billy gave the guy a departing smack and we ran like hell. I never saw Billy and Yac get into the car because I just kept running until I reached Orange. Oh what a night that was. This was the kind of stuff I was up to. I was going everywhere and nowhere—fast.

Chapter Five

The Sicilian Mafia

The Sicilian Mafia was the broker for much of the world's heroin and co-caine. The Sicilian Mafia was the only organized crime syndicate that had the mechanism to move heroin and cocaine across continents and oceans in large quantities. Sicily's Men of Honor held strategic outposts from Bangkok, London, Munich, and Marseilles to Montreal, Caracas, Sao Paulo, and some twenty-five American cities.

Prior to 1957, the American Mafia prospered from their gambling operations and their infiltration of the labor unions. There was very little enforcement, and their operations had no interference until the United States passed the Narcotics Control Act and created the Federal Bureau of Narcotics that later became the Drug Enforcement Agency (DEA). This was the result of Senator Estes Kefauver's Special Committee on Organized Crime's hearings that exposed the Mafia as a sinister nationwide crime syndicate that specialized in the sale and distribution of narcotics.

For the first time, the Sicilian Mafia was under attack by law enforcement in this country. It was then that the agreement was made between the Sicilian Mafia and the American Mafia.

Carmine Galante, a member of the Bonnanno crime family who later became the short-lived Boss of the same family, was sentenced to twenty years in prison for trafficking in drugs. Galante, who ran the operations of his family from prison, was able to strengthen his position at the same time, and he disregarded the new rules and continued trafficking in drugs. After his release from prison, he was assassinated while eating linguine and clams. The "hit" was sanctioned by the "Commission" for violating the rules of the American Mafia. Vito Genovese, the Boss of the Genovese crime family, was also arrested and sentenced to fifteen years for dealing in drugs.

In New Jersey, Tommy Campisi and Jerry "the Boot" Gallicchio were the first to bring heroin into the Newark area and were among those arrested and incarcerated by the newly created DEA. Their siblings continued dealing in drugs for another fifty years.

I always received great satisfaction from arresting members of these renegade families. You see, when I got married and broke away from the old neighborhood is when narcotics first hit the streets of Orange. Old friends of mine who didn't drink alcohol or even smoke cigarettes became hooked on heroin. Billy Smuggler and Anthony Yacovino both OD'd on heroin. That was it for me. I never went back.

Chapter Six

Drugs Hit Orange

The mid-fifties brought Rock and Roll and drugs. I heard about friends of mine from the other side of town and in Newark using marijuana and heroin, but I still had not been exposed to any drugs. Orange was changing. When you walked through the heart of Little Italy on Essex Avenue, you no longer saw the wooden portable shack where you could buy homemade Italian Ice in any flavor, yes, even chocolate. The little man with no legs who wildly ran his skateboard throughout the neighborhood was no longer around. I heard a car finally hit him. Where did Bacala go? No one could play the spoons like Bacala. He actually had spoons with lights on them. What a show he would put on in the dark. He was also noted for being the fastest clam shucker in all of Orange. Pizzerias were popping up all over. Sure, the Italian bakeries were still there, and occasionally you would see someone leaving a bakery carrying a crusty Sicilian Pizza that was just made old country style in the coal-fired clay oven. On holidays, many turkeys would be baked in those ovens. The Italian YMCA was knocked down to make room for Route 280, and the projects were being built for the lower income blacks. Many Italians started moving west into West Orange and the Hanovers. Angelo "Gyp" DeCarlo, a Caporagime in the Genovese crime family and his soldier Dan "Red" Cecere could still be found at the Berkeley Lounge on Essex Avenue, and the Genovese Club on Day Street was still active, and there were still wise guys hanging out in front of both places. Something else was happening. In 1951, United States Senator Estes Kefauver (Dem. Tennessee) held hearings in Washington DC, and his committee for the first time identified a national criminal syndicate called the Mafia and identified their criminality as narcotic traffickers. In 1956, the Narcotics Control Act was created and the Federal Bureau of Narcotics was formed to combat drug trafficking. As a direct result, about four hundred Sicilian Mafioso were deported and over two hundred Mafia gangsters were jailed, including Vito Genovese, whose organized crime family still carries his name. The American Mafia didn't need this heat brought on by the Sicilian Mafioso. The American Mafia had all the good rackets, such as gambling, loan sharking, labor racketeering, extortion, and infiltrating legitimate businesses, such as trucking, garment, garbage, construction, and the port industries. From October tenth to the fourteenth in 1957, the then Boss of Bosses, Joseph Bonnano, met with the Sicilian Mafioso at the Grand Hotel des Palmes in Sicily and an agreement was made for the American Mafia to separate from the Sicilian Mafia. The Sicilians were given the U.S. franchise for the importation and distribution of heroin to the United States, and the Sicilian Mafia would not infringe on the American Mafia's rackets. The Sicilian Mafia knew that even though an agreement was made, the American Mafia would use their police contacts to crack down on the Sicilian drug traffickers. When Bonnanno returned to the U.S., there were meetings across the country to outline the new rules of the American Mafia. The American Mafia would outlaw trafficking in narcotics, prostitution, bombings, and attacks on law enforcement officers. Joseph Bonnanno felt that all the activities of the Sicilian Mafia would bring down the American Mafia, and he proclaimed that any violation of these new rules would be punishable by death. Joseph Bonnanno referred to this reorganization as "this thing of ours," or "our thing." The Cosa Nostra was born. The heads of all five New York families met at the house of the Boot Bioardo. Only Albert Anastasia defied Bonnanno, and he was murdered on November 12, 1957. Two days later, on November fourteenth, representatives of the Cosa Nostra met at the infamous home of Joseph Barbaro in Apalachin, New York. A New York state trooper recognized the meeting and the house was raided. The publicity about the raid further showed that a national organized crime syndicate existed in the United States. Many experts have varied opinions as to the reason for this gathering, but the truth is that this was the birth of the Cosa Nostra and the establishment of the new rules of conduct. Well, I saw change after that. Heroin from Sicily hit the streets in the mid-fifties. First in the black neighborhoods, and then in the low-income Italian neighborhoods.

Chapter Seven

Apply to State Police

The best thing that ever happened to me was when Pris and I got married. Yes, we were only eighteen years old and within the first year of marriage had our first child, our son Chris. My parents wanted me to go to college, but our early marriage removed that option. I was a pretty decent mechanic, so I used our wedding money to open a gas station in Clifton. I went broke in a year and was fortunate to get a job at a respected garage, Beckman's. Becky and his two sons, Bruce and Charlie, treated me well, but I wasn't happy. Home was in Orange and Becky's was in Clifton, over a thirty minute drive. It was hard making ends meet. In order to make seventy-five hundred dollars a year, I would work at a gas station from opening at 6:00 a.m. until 9:00 a.m. and then work at Beckman's Garage from 9:00 a.m. to 6:00 p.m. six days a week. After 6:00 p.m., Bruce and I would simonize cars at twenty-five dollars per car for extra money. One day I went into the garage's office area, and there was a newspaper opened on the desk with a large ad reading, "State trooper test tonight at 7:00 p.m. sharp at William Patterson College." I didn't even know what a trooper looked like, but I figured, what the heck, it had to be better than what I was doing.

I went and took the test without telling anyone about it. I didn't think I had a chance, because I heard that twenty-five thousand men were to take the test statewide to enter into a class of sixty. Despite the odds, I passed the test. The second phase was the physical/medical exam. I was in great shape, so I thought I would do fine. The phase after that was a field interview by an SP Detective. The cat came out of the bag when a state police detective walked into Beckman's and, after he identified himself, asked for me. I asked him if we could speak outside, so we sat in his unmarked police car and began the interview.

That year, some Ford vehicles had a motor mount defect because they would break off and drop the motor. They could not be fixed; they had to be replaced at the dealer's. We were getting a lot of Fords with this problem since we were located close to a Garden State Parkway exit. We figured out a way to tack weld it back together temporarily so that the driver could get to a local Ford dealership, which meant we made the car drivable for only a few miles. Well, don't you know it, the owner of a car I had done the temporary fix on came back shouting, "Hey mother fucker, I want to talk to you!" I was thinking, "Here we go," but I tried to be very polite, considering the fact that I was being interviewed for the state police and this clown was going to blow it for me. Well, the car's owner was a black man, and I responded by saying, "I will be right with you SIR," hoping he would pick up on the fact that I was in the middle of something very important. It didn't work, because he started banging on the troop car, shouting, "Mother fucker, I want to talk to you right now!" That was it. Out of the car I go and I throw the guy right over the car and shout, "I'll show you who the mother fucker is," adding, "Come back and I will kick your ass!" I thought for sure I blew any chance I had with the state police, but when I got back into the car, the detective told me he was done with the interview. Anyway, I made it to the next phase, which was to go before the board. Years later, I met that detective's sons. They both became state troopers too, and they told me that their father, who had passed away, always told that story about when he met with me. The fact was that he liked the way I handled the situation and concluded that I would be a very good New Jersey state trooper.

Chapter Eight

Academy

On June 20, 1962, I entered the New Jersey State Police Academy along with fifty-nine other men. Only twenty-five made it to the graduation. Pris was home with Chris and was pregnant with our second child. Good thing they were in an apartment right below my parents. Knowing that they were in good hands gave me piece of mind so I could concentrate on my training.

Every one of the recruits had a military background except for me. The first day, a lieutenant was showing us the proper treatment of the American flag. He asked the recruits how many of them were in the Marines, then the Army, Navy, and so on. I tried to hide but I couldn't. I was set up because he looked at me and went through all the branches of the services again one by one, asking me if I was in any one of the services. He then asked me if I was in the Boy Scouts and I replied, "No sir." Then he asked me about the Cub Scouts. Finally, I replied, "Yes sir, troop II , Orange, New Jersey." I was placed in the one-man "Goon Squad," which meant I had to march by myself yelling out cadence. I did this for about a month. Training was tough. I had a difficult time with the six-mile run. I was falling way behind and thought for sure that I was going to get thrown out because of it. Another recruit, Frank Carpanetti, a strong Marine who was sharp as a tack, took me under his wing. He made me stay up front next to him during the run, and when I started to slow down, he would grab my arm and force me to stay in front. Poor guy, he had to work twice as hard. He started throwing up at the end of the run. I felt so bad to see him like that. It motivated me to keep up and I never fell back again. The academy was a real grind.

I got called to the office one day and I was terrified. No one gets called to the office unless they are going to be kicked out. When I got to the office, all of the instructors were in the room.

I started shaking but was soon confused when they told me that there was a phone call for me. When I picked up the phone, my sister was on the other end. She was calling me to let me know that Pris gave birth to our second child, a girl, who we named Toni Anne. The Commander gave me a four hour leave to go visit my wife and meet my newborn daughter. I was so grateful and elated, but was wondering how I was going to make it. You see, it takes at least an hour and a half each way from Trenton to Orange. If I was going to do this, I had to hustle. I drove like a madman, arrived at the hospital, kissed my wife and baby, and then said goodbye and hit the road back to Trenton.

Chapter Nine

Becoming a Trooper

Well, I finally graduated and had to report to Morristown Headquarters for assignment. Well, I finally made it. I became a New Jersey state trooper on October 28, 1962. I could just imagine what the guys from my old neighborhood were going to say. Unbelievable. But this was a very proud moment of my life. My father and mother and my immediate family were thrilled. I was finally going to make something of my life. This was a great start. I was on the right track on what I and my family wanted me to do with my life. I was one of the twenty-five that graduated from a class that started with sixty recruits. The sixtieth graduating class of the New Jersey state police. I joined a force of about twelve hundred at a starting salary of four thousand, three hundred dollars per year, and we had to live in the barracks, receiving fifteen day passes each month. When I joined the force there were only two black troopers and no females. My first assignment was the Washington barracks in rural Warren County, approximately forty miles from my home in Orange. It was some experience. A city boy in farm country. When I reported for duty, I entered the barracks and there was a trooper at the desk wearing long johns, chewing tobacco, and spitting into an empty beer can. I saluted and reported, "Trooper Robert Buccino reporting for duty, sir." He responded, "Jesus Christ! Not another guinea lover!" He then pointed to a bedroom and told me that was my room but he did not have a pillow for me, and for me to try to put my uniform on correctly and to report back to him when I was ready. In those days there wasn't any field supervision. They simply assigned a car you and you went out and broke your cherry on your own. He was right; it took me about a half hour just putting my uniform on. I was lean and mean and really sharp in uniform. Everything was perfect. I had decided right then and there that I wasn't going to let ethnic remarks affect my career. I would have time to deal with their prejudices. I will never forget that day. After I was properly dressed, I reported back to the duty trooper. I learned later that he was on light duty with a terminal illness and that he really wasn't a bad guy. He just liked to bust balls. When I came out, he told me how "pretty" I looked and threw me the keys to #476, a black-and-white '62 Ford. They were standard shift, no radio, no air conditioner, and we had to wear our hats in the car. That wasn't easy. He told me to leave the barracks, make a right turn, and patrol until I reached the sign for Hackettstown, which was the end of our patrol area. Then I was to turn around and drive until I came to a sign that said "Welcome to Pennsylvania," which was the end of our area. I left the barracks and wasn't five minutes away when I came upon a head-on collision. I totally panicked. There were serious injuries in both vehicles. I called for all assistance like they instructed us to in Motor Vehicle Accident Investigation class at the academy. I requested trooper assistance and the identification unit to take photographs, an ambulance, and the medical examiner. The only thing I received was the ambulance, and that seemed to take forever to arrive. I approached the first car and there was a woman who appeared to be in shock. I knew I had to keep the injured warm until medical assistance arrived. I checked the other car, and the driver had a piece of glass sticking out of his eye. I told him not to touch his eye and that I would be back. I opened the trunk of the troop car looking for a blanket and first aid kit, only to find a rusty World War II first aid kit. I opened it and a three-by-five packet that contained a small paper blanket. I had to keep that woman warm. Traffic was stopped in both directions. I shouted out to see if anyone had a blanket. A bystander said that they had a blanket but that it was gift wrapped. I confiscated the gift, removed the blanket, and placed it on the injured woman. Still no help. I kept running back and forth from the two vehicles, trying to help the injured. The woman seemed to be improving with the blanket and was talking to me. I went to check on the man with the glass in his eye and he was down and out. Shit! Now he was in shock. I took the blanket off of the woman and placed it on the man. Then I remembered our orders when investigating accidents. We had to give someone a ticket. So I removed the wallet of the injured man to get his driver's license and started writing a ticket for careless driving. The ambulance arrived and they were beginning to take the injured. I told them to wait a minute so I could finish writing the ticket. I placed the ticket on the chest of the man as he was being taken away. What a cluster fuck. I don't think that ticket was ever paid. When I finally cleared the scene, I received a radio transmission to return to the barracks to do the accident report. When I returned, the senior trooper, Bob Parango, who acted as if he was a brigadier general, greeted me. He made it perfectly clear to me that he was the Boss and next in line to become a sergeant. The station commander in those days was the rank of sergeant and could be considered equal to a chief of police title. I felt kind of relieved because the senior trooper was Italian and was originally from Newark, so he gave me some encouragement. He told me he was going to take me for a ride to show me the area. He drove, and as he would pass an intersection he would say things like, "This is Pistol Creek Road," or "This is old turkey brook lane." Of course I didn't remember one thing he told me. As we were driving through Little Washington, he shouted, "There's that son of a bitch!" He then sped up, pulled alongside a car being driven by a white male, and pulled him over. He wasn't telling me anything. I thought that this must be a wanted man. Probably for armed robbery or maybe even murder. He got out of the car and I followed. My hand on my six-inch Colt revolver, you know, just in case. Parango literally pulled the man out of his car. He didn't handcuff him and threw him in the back seat of the troop car. He ordered me to park his car, lock it, and take the keys. He then told me to drive back to the barracks. He got on the radio and called two other troop cars, advising them to meet him at the barracks and that he "got that guy." As I drove back to the barracks, Parango kept reaching back giving the guy a couple of smacks. When we got back to the barracks, the two other troopers were there waiting along with the trooper on desk duty. They ordered me to hold down the desk while they took the guy into a back room. I heard them shouting at the guy, saying, "The next time you tell someone where you work that you saw a trooper cheating on his wife, you won't be able to walk out of here." He continued, "My wife works there and heard your story; that's all we need is someone like you causing family problems for one of our troopers." After smacking him around a little more they told me to drive the guy back to his car. I didn't say a word. I still couldn't believe it, but I didn't mind it either. It showed me that I was in an organization that protected its own.

A true brotherhood. The guy must have said one hundred times on the way back to his car that he was sorry and that had great respect for the troopers and never meant to cause any problems for any trooper. That evening, I was given the 8:00 p.m. to midnight patrol and was expected to answer calls from midnight to 8:00 a.m. I was given a call regarding a child abuse complaint. When I went to the house, the father was nasty and wouldn't allow me to enter the house. I called the barracks of the potential danger and within minutes every trooper in the barracks was there to assist me. That was the way it was. You could always count on the troopers to be there for you. When there was a job to be done, it was done.

After the first day, I was already broken in. The next day I woke up and put on my uniform and tilted my hat. I was already an old salt. The governor had just named the first Italian superintendent of state police, Colonel Capello from Bergen County. Like all new Bosses, he visited every barracks to meet the troopers. When he visited the Washington barracks, the place was spit shine clean, and we stood at attention as he gave us a pep talk. He approached me and put his arm around my shoulder, calling me by name, and he asked me how I was doing and told me if I ever needed anything to call him. After he left, the sergeant and the other troopers asked me if I knew the colonel who in the state police was like God. Being slick, I figured I might as well take advantage of the situation, so I said, "Know him? He's my uncle." That was it. I could never take that statement back. Even the sergeant started to brownnose me. He would say thing like, "Don't forget when you see your uncle, tell him this barracks is well run." Parango actually asked me to speak to the colonel about a promotion.

Every trooper in the barracks chewed tobacco. If you've ever seen someone chew, it looks good. So, wanting to be one of the guys, one morning I stopped at a country store. As I entered into the front of the store, I saw a whole rack of different chews. I saw one called apple. Looked pretty good to me, so I bought it. There were a group of hillbillies in the store and I introduced myself as the new trooper in the area as I bit into the chew. After one unintentional swallow, I was on my knees gagging. I rushed to my troop car and, with my head hanging outside the window throwing up, the last thing I remember is those hillbillies belly laughing. Then one day I received a call to go to a farmhouse and see a Mrs. Smith about a complaint. I was about ten miles away and, not knowing the nature of the complaint, I sped to the house. As I entered her long driveway at a high rate of speed, I ran into a group of geese, probably killing two or three. I wasn't going to worry about it and just continued to the farmhouse. An elderly woman, Mrs. Smith, greeted me. I introduced myself. "I'm Trooper Robert Buccino; what seems to be the problem, and how can I be of assistance to you?" Mrs. Smith answered, "Trooper, you have to do something about the speeders. They're running into my geese and ducks and killing them." Red-faced, I assured her that in the future, my presence would be seen in the area to reduce the speeders on the roadway. (It would be funny if she'd said, "Yeah, I saw a few on my way in.")

Another time, I received a call to see a very upset farmer. When I met with him, he was loading a shotgun. I asked him what the problem was and he said, "It's the god-damned Heffers," and pointed to his neighbor's farm. He said they keep coming onto his property and causing damage, and that he was going to shoot them the next time. I told him that he couldn't take the law into his own hands and that he should go to the municipal building and sign a complaint for trespassing against the Heifers, and once the complaint was signed, I would arrest them. He gave me a puzzled look and asked, "You will actually arrest the Heffers?" To which I replied, "I certainly will." He thanked me and I went on my way. When I returned to the barracks, I submitted my report, advising the procedure in the arrest of the Heffers. After reading the report, one of the senior troopers told me to take a ride with him. He brought me to a farm and started pointing at cows. "That's a Jersey, that's a Guernsey, and that's a Hereford." How was I supposed to know that he was talking about cows? I thought that Heffer was the last name of his neighbor. I guess you can take the boy out of the city, but you can't take the city out of the boy.

After the first nine months at barracks, the entire class would be transferred to another barracks. It would usually take about two years before they would bring you to a barracks close to where you resided. It was very unusual, but I was transferred to Little Falls, which was the closest to my home.

Chapter Ten

Little Falls Barracks

The day I reported to Sergeant Charlie Bow Wow, he greeted me by saying, "So, you are Cappy's nephew." Now it made sense. This was a great station with a group of great troopers, and Charlie Bow Wow was the greatest. It was primarily a traffic station, and we were expected to write a lot of tickets, which was something I didn't have the heart to do. But, it wasn't a problem. There were troopers like Wicky Wacky that would write over one hundred tickets a month, so when I was on leave, I would just leave my summons books on my dresser in the barracks and when I would return to duty, Wicky would have about twenty tickets written in my book. Wicky was into racing pigeons, and it wasn't unusual to go into the barracks kitchen and see Wicky operating on one of his pigeons. One morning, in the middle of rush hour, there was an abandoned car locked in the middle lane of the highway, causing a major traffic jam. I had called for a tow truck when I saw a Chinese man running toward me and yelling that it was his car. When he approached me he said, "Please trooper, don't tow my car. I own House of Lam. Please be my guest for dinner," and handed me his card. It made sense to me now that he was there to just push the car to the shoulder and skip the ticket. In those days, we ate our meals in the barracks even though most of the restaurants in the area invited us for dinner. That same evening, Sergeant Silver Fox asked me what we were going to do for dinner and I told him about the invitation I received for Chinese food. So that's where we decided to go. We took a booth, but I didn't see the Chinese guy from earlier. We ordered chicken chow mein because it was the cheapest dish on the menu. After we completed our dinner, the Chinese guy came out of the kitchen, shook my hand, took the check, and said, "Dinner on house." We thanked him and left. A couple of weeks later, the sergeant suggested we go back to the same Chinese restaurant, and we did. This time, I saw the Chinese guy and he came over and shook my hand again. This time, the sergeant ordered Lobster Cantonese. I ordered the chicken chow mein again. After we finished our dinner, the Chinese guy came over to our table, again thanking me, picked up the check, and said, "Ice cream on house," adding, "Best can do." Boy was the sergeant mad. He didn't like spending money.

One night I was on patrol and it was raining very hard. I rolled up on two cars on the side of the road. Two men were lying face down in the mud and there were two men in plainclothes with guns drawn. I stopped and ordered the two men to identify themselves. They were New York Police Officers. They were surveilling two men suspected of pulling off post office burglaries in New York. They followed them into New Jersey. Not having a way to communicate, and being in their personal car, they simply continued their surveillance, which brought them to a post office in New Jersey where the suspects made an illegal entry. When they left, the officers decided not to wait for them to return to New York, but to arrest them in New Jersey. They pulled alongside the suspect's car and flashed their badges in an attempt to pull the suspects over. During this time, the officer driving the car fired two shots through the roof of his own vehicle. I called into the barracks and advised that I was bringing in two prisoners and was having the car towed there as well. Before leaving the scene, the two New York officers asked me for directions to the barracks and said that they would be right behind me. Charlie Bow Wow was in charge that night and always had an Italian stogie in his mouth. When I brought the prisoners in, Charlie asked me what crime they had committed and who the arresting officers were. I didn't know either answer. I can swear that Charlie swallowed his cigar. About an hour went by before the two New Yorkers finally showed up. They had obviously had stopped and had a few belts of whiskey. They carried into the barracks with two cases of beer and a couple bottles of whiskey. By the time the evening was over, Charlie Bow Wow was lying on the floor snoring and the two New York cops were bunked out in one of our bedrooms. Another job well done.

The Little Falls barracks was a great assignment, and I have great memories from there. On November 22, 1963 I had stopped a tractor trailer on

Route 46 in Little Falls and was in the process of writing the driver a traffic summons for an equipment violation when the trucker started blowing his horn and motioning me to come to his vehicle. When I asked him what was wrong, I noticed that he was crying. He told me that President Kennedy had been assassinated in Texas. I got into his truck to listen to the radio accounts of what happened. We were both crying. After about a half hour, I got out of the truck and gave the driver a hug and started back to my troop car when I remembered something. "Hold on a minute," I shouted. "I forgot something." I handed him a ticket for his equipment violation. Life goes on. I had met President Kennedy during the summer of 1963. The state democratic chairman was Sal Bontempo. Sal owned the Braidburn Country Club in Florham Park. President Kennedy played golf with Sal on one very hot summer day. Three other troopers and I were assigned to accompany the president and the foursome during their golf outing. We were ordered to stay with them at all times. Our trooper uniform was made of heavy wool, a long-sleeved shirt, and a tie. It certainly was not too comfortable in the intense heat. Some idiot decided that instead of using golf carts, they had two horse and buggies for the foursome to use. After they would tee off, they would get into the buggies and the horses would gallop down the fairway with four soaking wet troopers running alongside. The only thing I regret about the detail was that I never got an autograph or a photo with President Kennedy. At the time, I was just trying to survive. That country club has been part of my life for a long time. When I was a kid, I caddied at that course for two dollars a bag. I actually caddied for Sal Bontempo on one of my last caddying days. My friend Moon Mullins and I were caddying for Sal and his guests. At the end of the ninth hole, the foursome went into the clubhouse for lunch and never even offered us a drink of water, let alone lunch. Cheap bastards. To get back at them, when they were teeing off at the tenth hole, Moon gave the old cough routine. Sal Bontempo gave us a warning, but we did it again during his swing. We were thrown off the course. The next time I was there, it was with the President of the United States. I now play golf there. Life is strange like that.

In the early morning hours of a mid-August day in 1963, Thomas Trantino and Frank Falco murdered a Lodi Police Officer VOTD and a Special Police Officer TEDESCO in a nightclub in Lodi, New Jersey. I was the only trooper on patrol that night when I received a radio broadcast. I set up on the westbound lanes of Route 46. One of the first reports was that there were two subjects operating a Buick. Don't you know it, a Buick passed me going west on 46. The Buick was swerving and it appeared that the driver was intoxicated. We didn't have radio communication with the local police at the time, so I stayed behind the Buick until I reached the Caldwell area. At first the driver would not pull over when I tried to have him pull over. Although tension built up, I could see one person in the vehicle behind the steering wheel. A couple of truckers blocked the road for me. I got out of my troop car, gun in hand, and approached the car. The driver obeyed my orders and put his hands outside the window. I glanced at the backseat and saw that it was clear. Once I got him out of the car and cuffed him, I had him lay face down on the pavement and searched him. He didn't have any weapons on him. While the truckers watched over him, I went to search the car for weapons. There was a brown bag on the floor in the backseat area. I reached in the bag and there were live crabs. I almost peed my pants as I let out a shout. I found out later that the guy I arrested for DWI had been crabbing and sipping out of a bottle of Seagram's Seven during the evening and was not involved in the shooting of the Lodi cops. A couple of nights later, our state police detectives were in New York with NYPD detectives checking hotels for Falco and Trantino. I was on the book at Little Falls monitoring and recording every time a hotel was checked out. It was early in the morning when I got a transmission that Falco was found, shot, and killed. When the detectives came back, they told us that when they stopped at this one hotel and once Falco's photo and room were identified by the clerk, the New York detectives told our detectives to wait downstairs and that they would take care of Falco. Our detectives then heard a shout: "NYPD, freeze!" Bang, bang, bang. The next day, Trantino surrendered. I wonder why.

Chapter Eleven

Uniform Days

Garden State Parkway:

When a trooper had two years' road experience, he had to serve a minimum of eighteen months on a toll road. Most troopers did not want to leave life in the barracks. The problem was that once you were assigned to a toll road, it was very difficult to get transferred back to the road after you completed the mandated eighteen months. So, many troopers would submit a request for transfer as soon as they received their assignment to the toll road. On the toll roads, a trooper worked eight-hour shifts. I submitted my request for transfer as soon as I received my assignment to the parkway, although I kind of liked the assignment because it only took me ten minutes to get to work.

I played on both the softball and football teams. It was fast-pitch softball and I was the catcher. Our team was so good that we went undefeated. We played the state police teams of New York, Connecticut, Pennsylvania, Maryland, Massachusetts, Delaware, and at least a dozen local police departments. We played flag football, but it was more like tackle. Our big game was against the Turnpike. Quite a few troopers played college ball, and we had a couple that even played professional ball. I was in the tackle position, and it was a hard hitting position. Anyway, in the first quarter, I broke my thumb but couldn't come out of the game because my teammates wouldn't allow it, despite my pleas.

The state police did not sanction outside activities, especially football. I was on the eleven o'clock shift, so I went to work. My hand was hurting badly, and it was so swollen that I had a hard time putting my uniform on. I snuck past the sergeant because I couldn't button the sleeve. I figured I would go on patrol and tell the sergeant I tripped and fell, therefore reporting I got hurt on duty. There was no such thing as worker's comp cases in those days, so I wouldn't receive any benefit other than protecting our football team. So I went on patrol and pulled over the first speeder I saw. As I was asking for the driver's credentials, the driver saw I was in pain and asked me what happened. I told him that I slipped while approaching his car and apparently hurt my thumb. He asked me if he could help and I said that he could, by accompanying me back to the troop car to help me. You see, I couldn't write, and someone had to fill out the information on the ticket. I cut him a break for being such a nice guy and charged him with a non-moving violation. He thanked me for the break and I thanked him for writing his own ticket.

Education was not important in those days, and very few troopers had college educations. My cousin was a professor at Seton Hall and contacted me. Seton Hall started a pilot program, a four-year criminal justice program. They couldn't fill a class, so they would give me a four-year tuition scholarship. However, the classes were only offered during the day. I put in a request to change my shift so that I could attend. It had been a few weeks and I hadn't heard back from the top about my request, until one day while qualifying at the range, the lieutenant shouted out, "BOO-KEEN-O," (always pronounced my name wrong) "Front and center!" When I was in front of him, he continued, "So, you want to go to college? Listen, we will teach you everything there is to be a trooper. Request denied!" Soon after, money became available for law enforcement to attend college and practically everyone jumped aboard except me. One thing I am not is a hypocrite.

In 1964, I got transferred to the Garden State Parkway, and I heard that Tumac was now a man of respect in the Luchese crime family. The other families were starting to back away from the inner city numbers racket because of the Black Panthers' resistance to outsider whites controlling their neighborhoods. Only Tumac remained strong in the black neighborhoods of Newark.

I was assigned to the Garden State Parkway in 1964. In those days, every trooper had to serve at least eighteen months on a toll road. We didn't have to sleep at the barracks anymore. We now worked eight-hour shifts. If you lived close to the toll road like I did, it was a piece of cake. I lived in Orange and was only ten minutes from the station. I liked it and can tell a million stories.

I actually liked the GSP assignment. I was with a bunch of good guys and we all got along great. When we finished our shift at 11:00 p.m., we always went somewhere together. We got in trouble at home for it, but I survived. One night, we went to a nightclub on the Lodi Strip called the Pink Pussycat. We knew the owner and we would drink for nothing, and they would always have a good group. One night, there was a popular black group featured. The singer was amazing. She broke away from the group years later and became a global star. Her husband used to beat her, so she couldn't take it anymore and left him. After the show, the owner brought her over to our table and told her that we were all New Jersey state troopers. Then he told her to "show them your pussy." I almost passed out. I just got up and left. I don't know what the other guys did, but I could smell trouble and got the hell out of there as she was pulling up her short skirt.

One day in the early morning hours, a woman had a flat tire and stopped her vehicle in the fast lane, got out of her car, and was standing in the front of her car when another vehicle struck her car, pinning her underneath, and the fuel from the tank started burning. Another trooper and I were on the scene in seconds. The woman had a blond wig that had been knocked off her head, and the wig was in the full form and in the middle of the road. There was a scream. I thought she had been decapitated and gingerly walked up to the head, wondering how she could still scream. I gave it a slight kick only to realize that it was just a wig. I again heard the scream and saw the lady pinned underneath the car. The fire was small and hadn't reached her yet. A priest also stopped to assist. Trooper Carbone and I lifted the car while the priest pulled the woman from underneath the car. We became heroes. The other troopers kidded me for quite a while, challenging me to lift a car until the wheels left the ground. I told them I would when one of them came across a Studebaker, like the one the lady was pinned under. Sure enough, one of the troopers stopped a guy driving the exact make and model and called me to meet him. The challenge was on. I grabbed the left front fender with my back toward the car, and on several bounces was able to hold the car off the surface. I knew I could never do that again.

The Howard Johnson Restaurants on the Parkway were known to be hangouts for homosexuals. During the early morning hours one night, I responded to a report of a fire in one of the bathrooms of the Howard Johnson in the Township of Union. When I investigated the cause of the fire, I learned it was the product of a lover's quarrel between to gay guys. I received the name and address of the one who set the fire. He lived in the Ivy Hill Apartments in Newark, which was a large low-income apartment complex. It was about 2:00 a.m. and I proceeded to Ivy Hill in an attempt to locate and arrest him. This complex is a maze of apartments and I was trying to make sense of the numbers of the apartments when I came across a cab. I approached the cab driver for assistance and explained to him that there was a gay lover's quarrel and one of the men set fire to the bathroom on the Parkway Howard Johnson's and I was trying to find him. I showed the cabbie a piece of paper with the suspect's name on it, and the cab driver told me to follow him. He seemed very agitated and drove off in a hurry. He obviously knew where he was going and eventually pulled into a parking space. He got out of the cab and hurriedly walked into an apartment section. I followed with caution, thinking that this cab driver may be a kook. He took keys from his pocket and began opening an entrance door to one of the apartments. As we entered, there was a young man sleeping on a pullout bed. The cab driver pulled him from his sleep and started kicking the shit out of him. It was his son. I guess a statistician would give this a billion to one odds. You got to love this job.

Another time, one of the state troopers called the other cars in the area to meet him in one of the restaurant parking areas. When I arrived, the trooper was standing by a Chrysler whose windows were all steamed up. The trooper said, "Wait until you see this." When I looked into the car, I saw an elderly man in the driver's seat with his left hand reaching to the passenger side, fingering an attractive young lady. He was jerking off with his right hand. We knocked on the window and started opening the driver's door. The man didn't miss a stroke and kept fingering the girl but let go of his dick and tried to hold the door closed. He got all shook up when he saw we were troopers. The young lady was his secretary. We gave him the routine chewing out. "You should go to a motel and not use our parking lots for sex," we told him. He produced his identification and the trooper told him that he was going to let him go but that he was going to place his name in our sex files, so it better never happen again. There was no such thing as a "sex file"—it was just meant to scare him. Several hours went by and I was finishing up my patrol and did a final check of the restaurant parking lot when the same individual flagged me down. I asked him what he wanted, and he pleaded with me not to put him in the sex files. He was married and had several grown children and grandchildren and this was the first time he cheated on his wife of fifty years. I removed a blank piece of paper from my briefcase and tore it up, telling him that I would give him a break if he promised to never cheat on his wife again. He raised his right hand to God and made an oath. The poor guy was scared to death, and it probably was the first and only time he fooled around.

I was the only trooper to get off the Parkway in less than eighteen months. I was the early man, which meant that I would start my shift one hour before the next shift started, to assure proper patrol coverage during the shift changes. One chilly fall morning at dawn, I had just started patrol when there was a panicked radio transmission from one of the toll collectors calling for trooper assistance. Thinking that it was a robbery, I put the pedal to the metal and sped to the toll plaza. As I approached the plaza, I observed the toll collector standing by a four-door Plymouth, waving his arms to get my attention. I pulled over, and with my hand on my gun I asked him what was going on. The toll collector was shouting, "Arrest him, arrest him!" adding, "He is a toll violator." I couldn't believe that this idiot made me rush thinking it was such a serious crime when it was a simple toll violation. As I approached the driver's side of the vehicle, I saw a middle-aged man who was a neatly dressed. He was even wearing gloves. The first thing the gentleman asked was what he had done wrong. I explained to him that he was suspected of committing a toll violation. I received his credentials and approached the toll collector to find out what happened. He told me that the driver threw a slug into the toll basket instead of a quarter. This is a disorderly person charge in New Jersey, so I asked to see the slug. I noticed right away that it was a Canadian half penny that was similar in size and appearance to the quarter. It was obvious to me that it was a mistake and that the driver simply mistook the coin for a quarter. I returned the driver's documents and told him to put a quarter in the basket and that he could go his merry way. The toll collector went ballistic. He started screaming, "You have to arrest him!" adding, "There are directives from the director of the Parkway to do so!" That pissed me off, and I started chewing the toll collector out and telling him that he should be retrained on the use of the police radio. He kept screaming that I had to make the arrest, and I totally lost it. I threw a punch at the toll collector, but he ducked and I missed. I then chased him across the lanes to the administration building, where he hid behind his supervisor. We had a shouting match and I left. At nine o'clock sharp, I received a call from the lieutenant and was chewed out for throwing the punch and ordered to return to the toll plaza and apologize to the toll collector and everyone else that was there and then go to the Parkway's headquarters and apologize to the director. I told the Lieutenant that I could not do that. He asked me if that was my final decision. I said that it was and I was transferred to the Scotch Plains barracks two days later. That was the best thing that could have happened. I guess it's true that everything happens for a reason.

Scotch Plains

Once again, I had to live in the barracks, but it was an excellent duty. Warren Township in Union County did not have a police department, so the state police had full responsibility to provide police services to that community. The Scotch Plains barracks was an old house located on Route 22 in Scotch Plains. The troopers were like family. We did everything together. We were brothers. There were no women in the state police at the time, and very few minorities. One of the sergeants was named Alfie Uker. He weighed about three hundred pounds, and boy could he eat! What a great guy, such a character. All the troopers would try to go out on patrol before Alfie would wake up, because if you were still in the barracks, you would get the job of tying his shoes for him. He wouldn't be on duty for five minutes before you would get a radio call to pick up a package at "Chubby's Restaurant." The package would consist of about six sub sandwiches and a case of beer. The sergeant was hungry. A buffet had opened up across from the barracks, and the troopers had a standing invitation to eat there any time for free. Most restaurants knew we lived in the barracks and were grossly underpaid, so they would invite us to eat with them for free. They liked the presence of a trooper in their restaurants. We took Alfie to the buffet one evening only to get a phone call from the owner barring Alfie from the buffet because he ate pounds of roast beef. He was unbelievable. The food he would consume and the amount of beer and scotch he would drink during the day was enough to satisfy an army. Yet I never saw him drunk or screw up on the job.

One day I received a call in regards to a possible illegal entry. I met with a young couple at their newly purchased home and was told that they lived in Jersey City, had purchased this home, and were remodeling it on weekends. When they arrived this weekend they noticed that the snacks they had left on a coffee table had been eaten and that there was a mess. I asked them if anything had been taken or if there were any signs of a break in. They said they hadn't noticed anything missing but that there was a basement window open when they arrived. I told them that it was apparent that an animal such as a raccoon got in through the open window and had a feast, and that being from the city they would have to get used to all the little animals in this area. Imagine me giving advice on country living. We had a cup of coffee together and I told them to feel free to contact me if they needed anything. I went back to the barracks and about an hour went by when I received a phone call from them. "Trooper Buccino, we thought you would like to know that your raccoon stole our nineteen-inch portable television from our bedroom."

Another time, I was scheduled to go off duty at 8:00 a.m. after a three-day stint when the serge woke me up at 5:00 a.m. and told me to respond to a neighbor dispute. I couldn't believe it, a neighbor dispute at 5:00 a.m.? On goes the uniform and away I go. As I arrived at the complainant's house, I heard a continuous loud dog barking coming from a neighbor's side porch. That had to be the complaint, so I went to the neighbor's house first. When I looked into the porch, I noticed two large speakers blasting a recorded sound of a barking dog. I saw someone peek out a window and the recording stopped. I was pissed. Imagine playing a recording of a barking dog at your neighbor's house at 5:00 a.m. When I knocked on the neighbor's door, a man opened it and said, "He doesn't like it, huh?" He continued, "I work nights and have to sleep during the day, and he works days. When he goes to work, he ties his dog in the backyard and it barks all day when I'm trying to sleep, so I recorded his barking and I am playing it back to him while he's trying to sleep." I told him to make a pot of coffee and I'd be right back. I went over and got the complainant and we all had a cup of coffee and solved the dispute with understanding and laughter. That is what you call American ingenuity.

I still lived in Orange, and on my days off, I would visit a couple of my old friends. There was the barber, who was also a bookmaker, and the luncheonette where some loan sharking was going on, but they all knew my rule: "Don't let me see anything." When I walked into an establishment, it had better be clean. I would hate to lock up an old friend, but I would. There was an old friend, "T," who I knew was a bookmaker, and he had some status because his uncle was a made man. His wife, Helen, and mine were and still are very good friends. We had our class reunion and my wife had arranged for us to go with them. I told my wife I wouldn't associate with him, but I felt that since it was a class reunion, I wouldn't change her plans. We had a good time, but after we left the reunion, he suggested that we stop at the Manor in West Orange for a couple of drinks. The Manor is one of the most exclusive restaurants in New Jersey. It was rumored that it was built with numbers money. When we entered the Manor, "T" was treated with respect by practically everyone. He introduced me as his state trooper bodyguard. I got pissed and told him that I wanted to leave. I didn't say a word, but my blood pressure must have been off the charts.

We left and drove to the Clairmont Diner in Verona and pulled up to valet parking. The parking attendant approached the car and "T" asked him who he was turning his action in to and that he would send someone to see him soon. That was it. I grabbed him by the throat and if it wasn't for our wives being there, I would have decked him. I told him that he was not allowed to ever talk to me or walk on the same side of the street and if I ever had the chance, I would lock him up. He said I was thin-skinned, but for the next twenty years, he crossed the road when he saw me. He did eventually get locked up and did some time, and years later we did talk, but by then he was a different person. His wife eventually divorced him and I haven't a clue what happened to him.

On June 24, 1967 I was assigned to a detail covering the Presidential Summit at Glassboro State College. Glassboro was a small South Jersey college that was hosting the summit of President Johnson and Soviet Premier Alek. N. Kosygin. The temperature that day was in the high 90s, one of the hottest days of the year. The troopers, in their heavy wool, long-sleeved shirts, and ties were put on busses at 3:00 a.m. and given box lunches that consisted of dry cheese sandwiches. When we arrived at Glassboro, we reported to a hot gymnasium where we received our assignments. We went from detail to detail with little or no break time. By the afternoon, I was soaked from sweat and the inside of my legs were chafed. I just returned to the gym believing that the end was near and I would be able to take off my uniform and wash when I was assigned to my next detail, which turned out to be a beaut. Johnson and Kosygin were going to address the public in front of the dean's cottage. The state police, in all of their wisdom, fenced in a small area in front of the cottage's porch and corralled a couple hundred people. I was assigned to stand facing the crowd right in front of the president and Kosygin. I had about a three foot space between the porch and the fence. It was so hot that people started to pass out. When this happened, the crowd would lift the person over the fence to me. Believe me, there were no lightweights. I had to carry the person with wobbly legs about fifty feet to a waiting first aid unit. It was torture.

When this detail was over and we were marching back to the gymnasium expecting the final closure of this detail, we were stopped by Colonel David B. Kelly, the superintendent of the New Jersey state police. He instructed me to step out and follow him. He was with several Russians at the time. I followed as he and the Russians walked at a fast pace across an entire soccer field to a parking area where the colonel's black Buick was parked. He proceeded to open his trunk and there were two cases of Laird Apple Jack Whiskey which was made in New Jersey. I knew what was coming. I proceeded to carry the two cases across the soccer field, across the campus, to another parking area where the Russians had their car parked. The Russian opened the trunk of his car and I almost shit myself when I saw what was in there. Two cases of Russian vodka. They exchanged the booze and I had to carry the two cases of vodka back to the colonel's car. All in a day's work.

When I received a pass to go home, I stopped in the old neighborhood and saw some of my old friends. Nothing had changed. Some were still hanging out in front of the White Castle or in the clubs on Essex Avenue and Day Street. I heard that Tumac was on the rise in the Cosa Nostra. I always knew he had balls and was a tough kid, but I never expected him to be anything more than a street-level crook. I also heard that the East Orange-based Lucchese crime family's lucrative numbers racket in the black section of Newark was being attacked by the Black Panthers, who wanted control over their own neighborhood. It was rumored that Tumac was turned loose and had murdered several blacks and employed several blacks as controllers in his numbers racket. Remember Lenny Macaluso? We used to hang out together in Schimele's Pool Hall and the White Castle. I always knew him as a gambler. Well, he became a bookmaker and was one of Red Cecere's trusted lieutenants. The Genovese people under Caporegime Andy Gerardo still controlled most of the sports books and loan sharking in the areas of Bloomfield and the Oranges.

Caporegime Joe Paterno in the Gambino crime family was probably the most influential member of the Cosa Nostra in Essex County. He controlled the enforcement end of the Gambino crime family and the Boss of Bosses, Carlo Gambino. The Ironbound section of Newark was completely controlled by Anthony "Tony Bananas" Caponegro of the Philadelphia-based Bruno crime family. Carmine Battaglia, the Consigliare of the Colombo crime family, could always be found on South Orange Avenue in the Vailsburg Section of Newark. He was the mediator for the seven Cosa Nostra families operating in New Jersey. Boy, did he have his hands full.

The Campisis and the Gallicchios were renegades, pushing dope and conducting armed robberies. Sam the Plumber DeCavalcante was the Boss of the only New Jersey family. His family had strong influence over labor unions in New Jersey, and even though the Genovese family controlled the New Jersey Teamsters Union, if any made guy wanted to borrow money from the Teamsters, they had to go through Sam, who would then receive a commission.

Pizzerias were popping up all over, and there was a pizza war going on with the Columbo family and the Profaci's, attempting to take control over the services provided by their Italian food suppliers. New Jersey was unique. Even though there were seven families operating in the same area, they seemed to coexist. Of course there was an occasional war and a gangland murder from time to time, but all in all they seemed to work things out. After all, everyone was making money. Times were good for the Cosa Nostra. An example of this is that when there was a dispute between Carl Gambino, the Boss of the Gambino crime family, and Gerry Catena, the Boss of the Genovese crime family over the New Jersey and New York ports, it was decided that the Gambino family would control the New York side and the Genovese family would control the New Jersey side. Any family wanting to do business in the ports would have to seek permission from that controlling family. Organized crime was prospering in the early 1060s.

I was asleep on my last night of three days of duty at the Scotch Plains barracks on a hot summer night in July of 1967 when I and the other troopers were awoken by the sergeant and told that there was a riot in Newark and that we all had to report to the Roseville Armory in Newark. All of the troopers at the barracks in North Jersey, Troop B, were dispatched to Newark, and all the off-duty troopers were ordered to report to their barracks. In those days we had no riot gear. All we had were plastic helmet liners, our service revolvers, and several shotguns. With four troopers in a black-and-white, and because of our proximity to Newark, we were the first troopers in Newark. We got hit as soon as we entered Newark. Our windshield was blown out and we were under fire. I had the shotgun but I didn't return fire because I could not see who was firing at us. We were on the road all day and it was a real mess. Finally, late in the afternoon, we were ordered to return to the armory. When we arrived, we were handed a wool blanket and told to find a spot to sleep. My buddy, Trooper Ray Visconti, snuck into the officers' quarters to escape the confused racket that was going on in the armory. We took off our uniforms and sacked out on the couches. We were soon awakened as the colonel and his staff arrived. We snapped to attention and received the nastiest look from the lieutenant and were told to leave. The colonel countered the order and told us to stay and relax, so Ray and I sat in our shorts while the colonel held his first briefing. He asked the troop commander, Captain McElroy, to initiate the briefing. The captain put a map of Essex County on the wall upside down. He started to point to an area he called the Newark area, but he was pointing to Livingston, and he said that he had about three hundred troopers assigned to Newark when the colonel interrupted him and said, "Christ sakes, Mac, your map is upside down and you only have one hundred eighty troopers in all of Troop B. Sit down." I looked at Ray and I knew he was thinking the same as I—we were in trouble.

It was a hectic week. We had very little sleep and didn't have a change of uniform or underwear. On about the third day, reinforcements arrived. First Troop C, Central Jersey, under the command of Captain Babbick, a highly respectable gung-ho captain. Troop B troopers were still in the same uniform and were unshaven, smelly, and tired. We could hear Troop C's spit shined troopers arrive as they sharply marched under the cadence calling of Captain Babbick. They were followed by Troop A, South Jersey troopers. Very few know this about South Jersey. In the state police we called them the "sixty-niners" which was the area code for South Jersey. Anyway, the southern tip of New Jersey is south of the Mason-Dixon. It's a different world in South Jersey. You may know it as the Pineys. When the South Jersey troopers arrived, some were carrying rebel flags. The riot had simmered down some by the time they arrived, but almost started up again because of the attitude of the sixty-niners toward the blacks. On one occasion, a fireman had been shot and I was on the perimeter, enforcing the curfew, when an elderly black woman came out on the street calling for her grandchildren. I saw several South Jersey troopers raise their batons and I ran over and got in between. I asked here where her grandkids were and I assured her they would be okay. She went back into her apartment. I spent most of my time protecting the blacks from the troopers. The media reported that about thirty-eight blacks were killed during the riot. I heard that some of the bodies found were the work of Anthony Acceturro in his effort to maintain control over the numbers business.

The rioters didn't go into the Italian sections of Newark, which were greatly protected by the wise guys and Tony Imperial; a self-imposed guardian of the people. He had Tony's vigilante army on his side; they were an army of street toughs from Essex County.

After Newark, I went directly to Plainfield, where a new riot had started. I hadn't been home for over twenty days! When I finally went home, my wife told me that a man had come to our door when the riots broke out. He informed my wife that he knew I was a trooper and that I was in Newark, and that while I was away Tony's army would watch over and protect my family. He gave her a telephone number to call if she had a problem. Imagine that. The wise guys were protecting my family. I was confident that my family was safe because I had heard the Red Cecere's guys were armed with automatic weapons and had patrolled the streets that separated the black and white neighborhoods. I didn't think there would be anyone so stupid as to defy the Cosa Nostra's army.

After the riots, things returned almost to the way they were. Dr. Martin Luther King was the advocate of peace and had carried on several peace marches across the country. One day in March, Detective Bob Kitzler and I were ordered to meet Dr. Martin Luther King at the Abyssinian Church in Newark and accompany him throughout New Jersey as he was campaigning for his mule train march on Washington D.C. Our orders were, "He better not get hurt while in New Jersey." When Dr. King saw Detective Kitzler and me, I could tell he was frightened. Anyway, we stuck with him like glue. Everything went well. Just a couple of weeks later, on April 4, 1968 he was assassinated in Memphis, Tennessee. I often wonder if he was being stalked in New Jersey and Kitzler and I had something to do with deterring the action. I was just glad it didn't happen on my watch.

Riots were occurring across the country. In Newark, there were more fires than rioters. The state police assigned investigators to monitor the activities in the City of Newark. The Newark police department provided a small room with a radio so we could monitor the police radio transmissions. When it came my turn on a midnight shift, I saw the little room that was assigned for the troopers. I approached the tour Captain, Rocco Paradiso, and asked, "Is this any way to treat an Italian Trooper?" Rocco laughed and invited me to work with him. Rocco, according to the state police top brass at the time, could not be trusted because he was too close to organized crime. I later learned that it was the prejudices against all Italian-American police officers, especially if the officer received recognition for making a lot of arrests and received publicity. At the end of my career, I experienced the same innuendos. That evening I found out exactly what kind of police officer Rocco was. There was a major warehouse fire in the Ironbound section of Newark.

Rocco and I responded. We were standing across the street watching the fire-fighters on the roof fighting the fire when we saw one of the firemen fall through the roof and into the burning building. Rocco, without saying a word, ran into the building and pulled out the injured fireman. I didn't move. Rocco then brushed himself off and calmly came back over to me, not saying a word about what he had just done. I was more excited than he was. He didn't mention the incident or seek praise for his heroic action. He instantly became my hero. I learned a lesson that day that I would follow throughout my career, not to give credibility to rumor or innuendo. Judge an individual by my own personal observations and my own evaluation of the facts. From that day on, when someone would characterize someone as being in the Mafia or a mobster, I would always ask how they knew that. In most cases, there wasn't any credible information to support their allegation.

Chapter Twelve

Late Seventies, Early Eighties

In the late '70s I investigated an individual who was performing abortions. I built up a strong case and arrested Camillo Molinaro for abortion. He turned out to be a made guy out of Cleveland. The case was brought before a Grand Jury in Morristown and was no-billed. I wasn't even brought in to testify. This bothered me to no end because I knew it was a strong case. It was obvious to me that the case was fixed. I found out there was a warrant out of Passaic County on him for abortion. Early March of 1980 I found him. He was using the name William Martin and was living in a high-rise on Mt. Prospect Ave in Newark with a young wife and a new baby. I surveilled him to the Teamsters Union in Totowa. I walked in and saw him sifting behind a desk. It was apparent that he was working for the Teamsters. I walked over to him and placed him under arrest. He didn't recognize me and I didn't say anything about the Morris County arrest. I read his rights and he told me his attorney, George Franconero, was in the building, so I told him to call for him. I knew George, the brother of Connie Francis, and he was up to his neck in organized crime and had cooperated with the feds but refused protection. He was also involved in land fraud and fraudulent loans. He also testified before the New Jersey Commission of Investigation about Teamster Union dental plans. Anyway, he asked me what I had and I explained the warrant out of Passaic County. George then looked at "William Martin" and said, "You can trust Buccino. Go with him and cooperate. I will see you tomorrow." Wow. I was shocked, but it was okay with me and

I took him to the state police barracks in Totowa.

At first I asked him about the Morris County case, and just as I expected, he bribed his way out of that case. He said he gave $30,000 to a Democrat politician who had to give a third to a county detective, who also took a third to give to the state trooper, and the politician took a third for himself. Well, I was the state trooper and I know it wasn't me, so the county detective made a good score.

Then he started talking about the Teamsters. He laid out how money was going back and forth to Cleveland and Las Vegas. He was a world of knowledge and told me that he would cooperate completely as long as I kept him out of jail. We talked about relocation of him and his family, and he was definitely interested. It was getting late and I had to first keep him out of jail and then debrief him at length. I called the A.G.'s Office and spoke to a deputy A.G. I explained what I wanted to do, and that was to get a writ to place him in my custody, but the deputy wouldn't go along with it. He said that I would have to lock him up overnight and he would meet the next morning and we would get the writ then. I objected. I told the deputy that if the word that he cooperated got out, he would either clam up the next day or be dead. Well, I was right. The next morning we went to see Comillio Molinaro and he would not talk to us. I knew it would happen, and it did. They got to him overnight. We blew it.

Two days later, George Franconero, Connie Francis' brother, left his house in the morning and was shot to death by two assailants. I don't know if his blunder of letting Molinaro speak to me had anything to do with him getting killed, but it certainly appears that it was a factor.

There was a case developed by the state police in the '80s that was highly successful. It was the theft of construction equipment, backhoes, cranes, tractors, dump trucks. The mob from Bloomfield Avenue in Newark was making a lot of money stealing this equipment and shipping it to third world countries. Donny S. was a member of this group. He was a tough guy, and one of the charges against him, when the group was taken down by the state police, was threats made by him to an individual who owed money that he was going to throw acid into his face if he didn't pay the money. When he found out that he was getting a hundred year sentence, he decided to cooperate. He was prepared to testify against the entire organization, which included several made guys. He turned out to be a great witness, but he was hard to control, so the deputy attorney general asked me if I could handle him during the time that he was testifying. I agreed. In one of the difficult trials, he was outstanding, so the DAG told me to reward him by giving him anything he wanted to eat or drink. We had a room in a hotel in Morristown, so Donny and I settled down in our room. I had become quite friendly with Donny and was quite relaxed when with him. When we entered our room I removed my gun and put it in a dresser. I told Donny he could have anything he wanted, and he ordered a steak and a martini. Big Mistake. We both lay on our beds. Donny drank his martini and started eating his steak using his "steak knife." What I didn't know was that he had taken several pills before knocking down the martini. He became crazed. He jumped out of bed and with the knife in hand said, "Buccino, you're not taking me back to jail." He was right next to the dresser where I put my gun. He was closer than I. I tried to calm him down by speaking softly and trying to reassure him that he was getting a good deal from the state. As I spoke I walked slowly towards him. When I got close I hit him with a right punch to the jaw and knocked him down and grabbed the knife from him. He got up and was apologetic. He calmed down and I, of course, had my gun. Moments later, the trooper and DAG came into the room and asked, "Is anything wrong?" and I responded, "No, everything is great," and I never told them what happened. I always felt that they knew something happened but felt it in their best interest not to know. I don't think they know to this day.

Donny continued his cooperation, did a couple years in prison, and returned to New Jersey and, as far as I know, he has not been in trouble with the law or the wise guys. I will tell you the one thing that came out of this: I learned a big lesson. Always keep my guard up and don't get friendly with any informant or state's witness.

Chapter Thirteen

Vending Machines

It came to my attention from several sources that the Cosa Nostra had influence over and controlled most of the very lucrative vending industry. Especially Joker Poker machines. The Cosa Nostra had infiltrated the industry at the manufacturing, distribution, and territorial control of the video machines that were being used to gamble. I told my detectives that I wanted to focus on this industry, especially in Paterson, since that area was where I was receiving most of my information. I sent my detectives to several luncheonettes and taverns where there were these machines and noticed that not only did some stores have fifteen to twenty machines, all very busy, in the back rooms, but they also operated with impunity. Detective Ron Donahue came through again. He developed an informant who was in the industry. Interestingly, he was not operating illegally. At least to our knowledge he wasn't. Ron and I met with him and told him our game plan and asked if he would go into Paterson and try to get stops for his machines.

When he tried to place machines in Paterson, he was immediately met by an associate of the Cosa Nostra, John Ventura, and was told that if he wanted to place machines in Paterson, he had to pay Lucchese soldier Michael Perna, and he would also have to pay Patterson police officers for protection.

Wearing a wire, the informant recorded numerous incriminating conversations with several Patterson police officers and several members of the Cosa Nostra. It was very upsetting to me because I knew the officers arrested, and they appeared to be good detectives. Unfortunately, they took money.

The deputy attorney general prosecuting the case wanted me to testify and bring out the organized crime connection with the officers. I knew the judge would never allow an organized crime expert to testify, because the state simply had to prove the bribery and official misconduct, and the prosecution didn't need to prove they were involved in organized crime.

Well, there was a hearing as to whether or not they would allow my testimony. During my testimony, one of the officers' mothers died. I felt like crap. Ultimately, my testimony was not allowed. Detectives Casper Morelli and Raymond Zdanis were found guilty of accepting bribes of five hundred dollars and one thousand dollars per week and were sentenced to state prison. The third detective was allowed to resign from office after a hung jury. As a result of this investigation, Patterson passed an ordinance forbidding Joker Poker machines in Paterson. This was a large source of money for the Cosa Nostra, and they got a kick in the ass.

The informant and his family were relocated to Florida. He and his two sons were going to the beach every day with nothing to do. The father bought two wave runners, but they would only use them for a half an hour a day, so the father started to rent them and made a lot of money. With that money, he started buying old condos and renting them out. A highway was coming close to where he lived, so he wanted to go into the towing business. He needed a license from the local sheriff, but he had to give his identity. He chose to take the risk and signed a waiver for me to reveal his past to the sheriff. The sheriff turned out to be a good guy and understood the situation with the informant. He approved the license, and my last account was that the informant had six tow trucks and was doing great. He certainly made the right decision in helping law enforcement bring down organized crime.

In 1984, the Cosa Nostra made an attempt to take over the manufacturing of video poker vending machines in New Jersey. Vincent Craparotta, an associate of the Lucchese crime family, was beaten to death for refusing to extort money for the Lucchese family from hip nephews Vincent and Pasquale Storino. The Storinos were co-owners of SMS Vending Manufacturers Company in Point Pleasant. Anthony Accetturo gave the orders to kill Craparotta, and it was carried out by his subordinates.

After the homicide, Thomas Ricciardi, a soldier in the Lucchese family, went to claim SMS for the "family" only to find out from Storino that they were already with the Bruno crime family in Philadelphia. Storino told Ricciardi that Salvatore Mirando, their partner in SMS, had the association with the Bruno family. There were several sit-downs by the heads of the Bruno and Lucchese crime families over which family had the rights to claim the SMS vending company. The results of the sit-down were that the Storinos belonged to the Lucchese family and Salvatore Mirando belonged to the Bruno family, and he would pay tribute through Joseph Sodano, who was later murdered for not bringing the money to Philadelphia.

In 1993, justice was served. After a five-month trial, not only was Thomas Ricciardi found guilty of murder, but all the defendants were found guilty of racketeering and other charges.

Later that year, Anthony Accetturo and Thomas Ricciardi contacted me and offered their cooperation. As a direct result of their cooperation, Anthony Accetturo, Thomas Ricciardi, Michael Taccetta, and Michael Perna pled guilty to conspiracy to murder eleven people in furtherance of their racketeering enterprise.

This was a major blow to the Lucchese crime family in New Jersey. Not only did we wipe out the hierarchy of the "family," but we stopped their influence in the lucrative joker poker industry in New Jersey.

Chapter Fourteen

Spanky

I decided to move on, so I went up to Netcong in Morris County to work on a small crew that was controlled by John DeMattio, a local wannabe who was connected to Jimmy Higgins, a Gambino soldier, and later Michael Taccetta, a Lucchese Captain. DeMattio had everyone from Netcong, a predominately Italian neighborhood, intimidated. He ate, drank, and slept Mafia style. It was football season and football tickets were all over. This was a piece of cake for me since I was a controller myself when I was a kid and knew the M.O. by heart. On Saturday mornings, I would watch DeMattio because I knew his controllers would have to get everything in to DeMattio by noon. I identified all of his controllers. Then, on Friday evenings, I watched his controllers and identified his writers. On Sundays, I would watch DeMattio again to see when he was doing the work on the tickets. On Mondays, I again surveilled DeMattio and identified his supplier. When we raided, we arrested about fifteen guys and confiscated the weeks' work, which was about twenty-five thousand dollars. Not bad for one of my first jobs. I locked up DeMattio several times after and I tried to flip him. One day I received a call from him. He wanted to meet me and said I should come alone, and that we'd meet at the Netcong High School football field on the fifty-yard line. You won't believe it, but the Netcong High School football field was only eighty yards long. When a team would go on the offensive, they would have to move the ball twenty yards back to make up the distance. Anyway, we met mid-field. I thought for certain he was going to offer his cooperation, but instead he asked me if he could search me for a wire. I told him that if he touched me he would have to get his nose fixed. I said, "Get to the point. What do you want to do?"

He said, "How does fifty thousand sound to you?" I laughed and told him that I couldn't believe he was trying to bribe me. Especially since I knew he didn't have two nickels to rub together. I gave him a smack and left. A couple of weeks later, I arrested him again.

That wasn't the first time I was offered a bribe in Netcong. I locked up a bread man who was delivering Italian bread from Newark and had a numbers route that included Netcong. I arrested him, but it wasn't a big deal. There was a preliminary hearing and when I arrived at the courthouse. There was a brand new Cadillac in front of the courthouse, and the bread man was a passenger. I assumed the well-dressed driver was his attorney. He said, "Hi Bob, can't we settle this thing without going to Court?" and mumbled something about having to pay an attorney thousands of dollars. He offered me the "attorney fees" in exchange for dropping the case. I said, "Good try; I'll see you in court." After the hearing, I was outside talking to a couple of uniformed troopers when the Cadillac pulled up and again I was called over to the car. I asked one of the troopers to come with me in case I had to lock them up for bribery. The driver asked me, "Can we talk alone?" to which I answered, "You can talk in front of him." Then the driver said, "I know you won't take money, but how would you like to be worked over by two beautiful girls for the whole weekend?" adding, "Anything you want." I looked at the other trooper and said, "We'd better get out of here before I weaken." The bread guy wound up pleading guilty and got a fine and county jail time which was less than a year. I arrested over two hundred individuals for gambling offenses in a two-year period, and the newly created Organized Crime Task Force had arrested probably two hundred more. We were developing a hell of a reputation in the law enforcement and mob communities. I had arrested John DeMattio, a wannabe mob guy who was intimidating the citizens in western Morris County. John was a bookmaker and was in fact connected to Jimmy Higgins, a Gambino soldier, and later with Michael Taccetta, a Lucchese Capo. While I was testifying against him, the Task Force had a wire on a bookmaking operation in Essex County. During one of the court recesses, John called one of the Task Force targets and spoke to a bookmaker who I had also previously arrested and was awaiting trial. The conversation was about me. They said they knew where I lived and that I wasn't going to be around much longer. During my testimony, the room started to fill with troopers and Lieutenant Mike Gallagher, the CIS officer in charge. I had no clue what they were up to until I got off the stand and was told by Gallagher that the state police had sent troopers to my house to protect my family. My wife had been instructed not to let anyone in the house unless she saw his or her ID. Two troopers in civilian attire came to the door and identified themselves to my wife. They were carrying shotguns. We had a large Belgium shepherd at the time. When my wife opened the door and the dog attacked and tore the jacket sleeve off one of the troopers, who responded by telling my wife that it didn't appear that she needed protection as long as the dog was around. Against my protests, we had two troopers staying with us twenty-four hours a day. We must have cooked a hundred pounds of spaghetti. After over a week of being protected during the early morning hours, I was awoken by the sound of a car stopped in front of my house. I got my gun and walked down the hallway past the troopers' bedroom. They were snoring up an opera. I went outside to check the car out. They were just teenage lovers. The next day I called the lieutenant and strongly requested that the detail be terminated, and it was. Soon after, we made the arrests. At the briefing before the arrests, the lieutenant who gave the briefing instructed the team that was going to hit the house of one of the bookmakers not to use unnecessary force. He realized that a threat on a trooper would raise the emotions of the raiding party, but he warned us not to do anything, and to be sure we did, he was going to lead the raiding team. As it turns out, the lieutenant didn't take his own advice, because the team wound up having to pull him off of the prisoner as he was kicking the shit out of him. I didn't lay a hand on him, and when I went to court and faced him, he said to me, "You didn't have to give me a beating; we were only bullshitting." He obviously mistook the lieutenant for me. Whatever.

Spanky

Spanky was a real character. Frank DeFelice's nickname was Spanky because he looked just like the Spanky character from The Little Rascals. He had an extremely high I.Q., but he didn't like to work. He just liked to rip off anybody and everybody. From check kiting to passing fraudulent checks, he was a petty thief and was also involved with loan sharks and bookmakers. One of his best friends was John DeMattio, a wannabe. He had what he believed was a get out of jail free card. Whenever he got in trouble, he would cooperate with law enforcement. I was investigating several loan sharks and I knew Spanky owed them money. Spanky went to work for me. The loan sharks were heavy hitters, made guys like Jackie Adams, and Bucky Jones, a Lucchese crime family associate. Spanky had missed quite a few weeks' worth of vigs and I knew he was going to either get threatened or be given a beating. I set it up so he would meet them in a restaurant and I would monitor their conversation. Spanky carried a recorder and a transmitter so I could monitor in case it got too heavy and I had to intervene. Well, Spanky made the meet and I heard the conversation up until the point where they started shouting at him. The sound ceased. I didn't know what was going on and I had to make a decision to go in or not. I decided to wait. I almost had a heart attack when I saw two men carry a rolled up carpet out the back of the restaurant and load it onto a pickup truck. I thought, "There goes Spanky." I was ready to go in, when I saw Spanky leave the restaurant. We had arranged to meet at the Netcong state police barracks. While waiting for Spanky, I heard on the county radio that the Netcong Police, a two-man department, arrested Spanky on a bad check warrant. They would probably find the recorder and the wire on him if and when they searched him. I sent a trooper right over to the Netcong Police Department. The trooper told them that he would have to take custody of Spanky since there were other warrants. They never searched Spanky. He still had the equipment on him. By the time we got Spanky back to the barracks, the telephone and radio broadcasts were coming in from all over the county. There were over forty warrants outstanding for Spanky's arrest. It was Friday evening and Spanky did his best con job with me. He told me that tomorrow was his mother's birthday and that if I would let him go, he would turn himself in on Monday morning. I didn't believe him, but I felt he wouldn't screw me. Besides, I could always find him; he weighed over three hundred pounds.

In those days, the county prosecutor was a part-time job. The prosecutor would still have his law practice. Monday morning, Spanky was a no show. I reached out for him, but he was nowhere to be found. The Prosecutor's Office called, and I told them that I had him and that he was doing something for the state. I would surrender him in a couple of days. That bought me some time to find him. I went to every bookmaker in the area and threatened them with arrest. I learned that he might be with John DeMattio. I found John at his sister's home. His bags were packed and he was ready to go. I told him he was under arrest. He asked me what for and I told him that

I was going to decide on the charges soon if he didn't tell me where Spanky was. He proceeded to tell me that Spanky was in a hotel in Wayne and was waiting for John to pick him up. They had a plan to go to Vegas. I told John to go and that I would follow him. This way Spanky wouldn't know that John ratted on him. He would simply believe that I had John under surveillance. It worked like a clock. When John picked up Spanky, I pulled them over and arrested Spanky. I gave him one smack and brought him directly to the prosecutor's office. While there, I was told by a detective that the prosecutor wanted to see me. It was Prosecutor Egan, a great guy and excellent prosecutor, and later a judge. When I entered the prosecutor's office he said to me, "Mrs. Smith wants the car, dog, and a few thousand dollars. We would like to settle this thing." I had no idea what he was talking about, so I said, "Prosecutor, I'm Bob Buccino, a detective with the state police. I don't know what you are talking about."

Prosecutor Egan said, "Oh, that's right, you're a detective. I thought you were a judge and could release prisoners on their own recognizance." I definitely got his message.

While Spanky was in jail, I went to see him. While waiting for the guard to bring Spanky to the interview room, a security officer from Macy's came in to interview Spanky too. He told me that Spanky had passed a bogus check for merchandise and that he wanted to talk to him about restitution. I told the officer that he could go in with me and that I would let him go first. I had to see this. When Spanky came in, this guy started acting real tough, demanding that Spanky either give Macy's five hundred dollars or return the television. Spanky asked what kind of television it was and was told it was an RCA. Spanky thought for a while and offered him a Sears television instead. That was typical Spanky.

Chapter Fifteen

Anthony and Me

Who would ever believe that one day Anthony would become the Boss of the Lucchese crime family and that I would become the chief of detectives in the state's Organized Crime Task Force. We would begin together and end our careers together. We called him Tough Tony in those days. He was a tough kid, always wanting to hang around his older brother Rocco and me, but we would always chase him away. Their family owned a butcher shop down in the Valley section of Orange. Tony wanted to be a crusader in a big way, but we wouldn't let him in. I kicked him in the ass a couple of times when he would come around.

Tough Tony never liked the nickname "Dirty Feet" and I'm sure that if he reads this, he will be pissed. Years later, he reminded me of the times I threw dirt in his face. Back then, one would have thought that I was destined to be the wise guy, and Dirty Feet a laborer. We considered him to be a dumb kid. I don't recall if he attended school. I found out later that he wasn't dumb at all. He was a very wise man, not because he was well-educated, but because he was very astute and street smart. His brother Rocco opened up a construction company and a quarry and died at a young age. Rocco didn't want much to do with Anthony when Anthony decided on a life in organized crime. Dirty Feet and his family moved to East Hanover when he was in his pre-teens.

Anthony started to run with a street gang consisting of Gallichios and Campisis. They would rob and steal, and they specialized in breaking into vending machines and stealing the money. Hams Dolasco, a Lucchese soldier whose headquarters was on the corner of Sanford and Tremont Avenue in East Oranges, owned most of the vending machines. Anthony was the toughest and became the leader of this street gang. He was also a glom. He believed in taking anything he wanted from anybody at any time. If someone was eating a sandwich that he wanted, he would just walk up and take it from them and eat it. There was a movie released at that time called *One Million Years B.C.* featuring Victor Mature. It was about two cavemen tribes. Mature was from a tribe that was crude and ruthless, while the other tribe was more civilized, cooked their food, and shared their meals equally (the movie was released in 1967). Victor Mature was injured in a fight and was found and cared for by the more civilized tribe. When they were preparing a meal and serving it, Victor Mature's character just grabbed the meat from their hands and rudely ate it. When they tried to have him share the food, he pounded on his chest, shouting his name, "Tumac, Tumac." Since these were the same characteristics of Accetturo, he was from then on referred to as Tumac, a name that continues to this day.

Hams Dolasco, upset that Tumac's gang was robbing his machines, had Tumac picked up and brought to his club. Tumac stood up and defied Hams, so Hams felt that it would be in his best interest to hire Tumac to drive him and to do some leg breaking, so he gave Tumac a job with his organization—a job Tumac did quite well. However, Tumac wore two hats. One as leader of his street gang and the other as an assistant to Hams Dolasco. In the mid-fifties, drugs started hitting the streets. Jerry "the Boot" Gallichia and Tommy Campisi, Sicilian Mafioso, were responsible for the heroin in the area. Tumac's gangs were dealing the drugs primarily in the black neighborhoods, but many young Italians were also getting hooked. The police went to see Hams Dolasco and gave him a warning. As long as Hams was involved in numbers and loan sharking, the police would give him protection, but if that Tumac kid continued with his gang and with Hams, the police would no longer give him protection. Narcotics would not have police protection. Hams warned Tumac, but Tumac was defiant. One hot summer day, Hams, with his suspender pants and big belly, drove over to South Orange Avenue where Tumac and his gang were hanging out. He got out of the car and said to Tumac, "It's a hot day. Go get me an ice

cream." Tumac knew that he had a choice to make. If he went and got an ice cream for Hams, he would lose face with his gang, and belong exclusively to the Hams organization; or, if he refused, he would be out with Hams and may even be killed. He got Hams the ice cream and was on the road to becoming a made guy.

At the same time, I was in Orange running numbers and not knowing that the money I was collecting was going to Hams and Tumac. Life was pretty good for me at that time. I was hanging with the older guys, popular with the girls, had sharp clothes, bought a Pontiac convertible, and started dating the prettiest girl in town, who later became my wife.

Lucchese Crime Family

The Lucchese crime family was a powerful family whose base of operation was in the Vailsburg section of Newark, New Jersey. In the fifties, their North Jersey headquarters was a social club on the corner of Sanford and Tremont Avenues in East Orange. Hams Dolasco was the street Boss, and his brother Legs Dolasco, Vito and Lenny Pizzolato, and Andy Licari were his trusted lieutenants. The Capo regime during that time was Giuseppe Abate, who owned a winery outside of Atlantic City. The Lucchese family controlled a large amount of the lucrative numbers business in the central Newark and black areas of Essex County. It was in the fifties when I was asked to pick up a package from across the street from the Dolasco's club and deliver it to a house in East Orange. Of course it was a numbers package, but I was told not to look inside, and I didn't. All I got paid was three dollars for gasoline.

Anthony "Tumac" Acceturo was a young punk who was the leader of a street gang that consisted of the Campisis and Gallichios. His gang was involved in drugs and petty theft. They began breaking into vending machines owned by Dolasco. Dolasco had him picked up and brought to the club, and Tumac stood up to Dolasco. Dolasco took a liking to him and started using Tumac as his driver, and other "things." When Hams died, Tumac, knowing everything Hams did, took over the crew. He was the muscle for them, and the other members feared him, so they all stepped aside when Hams died. In the sixties, the Black Panthers attempted to take back the lucrative number business in the dominating black central ward and west side of Newark. Tumac made his move and it was rumored that several black numbers men were victims of unsolved homicides. One thing for certain was that Tumac and the Luccheses maintained control of the numbers business in the black sections of Newark.

In the seventies, the New Jersey State Commission of Investigations (SCI) began actively subpoenaing members of organized crime before their commission, compelling their testimony, and when they refused, they incarcerated them for being in contempt. The state police intelligence unit had the responsibility of preparing dossiers on the high ranking members of the Cosa Nostra for the SCI. I was assigned Tumac. One day while surveilling his Livingston home, I observed a truck backed up to his garage. I couldn't get the plate number, so I waited for it to pull out of the driveway, at which time I pulled close to his home to observe the license plate. When doing so, one of Tumac's guys came out and appeared to take down my plate number. I recognized "Rick" and actually stopped so he could get a better look at me. He got scared and turned around and ran back into the house. I followed the truck a short distance, and when I turned around I saw Tumac racing toward me in his green Lincoln Continental. When he passed me in the opposite direction, he gave me the "fist." This was like a keystone operation, because when I turned around to go after him he also turned around, and we once again passed each other in opposite directions. So I just pulled over to the shoulder and waited for him. I got my tape recorder and placed it under my seat. This was so that, if he threatened me, I would have the evidence to arrest him, but being all thumbs, I didn't press the correct buttons and it never recorded. When he approached my car, he recognized me and said "Buccino, why do they have you on me?" He then told me he had something for me and asked if he could sit in my car. When he sat in my car he offered me a bottle of "expensive" perfume for my wife. I told him to "forget about it." He asked me what I was doing, so I said that I had an SCI subpoena for him. This was just a bluff, because there wasn't a subpoena for him. He then said to me that he knew I had his phone tapped and that that there were bugs in his house. I knew there weren't any, so I told him he was correct, that every electrical receptacle in his house had a bug in it. I got a kick out of this, picturing Tumac and a team of electricians replacing all of the receptacles in his house the next day.

He was the driver, bodyguard, and enforcer for Peter "Hams" Dolasco, a soldier whose headquarters was on Sanford Avenue in East Orange. The Boss of the New Jersey faction of the Lucchese crime family was Giuseppe Abate, who resided in the Atlantic City area and owned a vineyard. Guiseppe was from the old school. He was made in the Sicilian Mafia and became Cosa Nostra in the late fifties. He ran his crew in the disciplined fashion of the Sicilian Mafia. The made members in North Jersey were Lenny and Vito Pizzolato, Joseph Licari, Hams, and Legs Dolasco. They ran a lucrative numbers business in the Oranges and Newark's west and central wards and paid six hundred to one on a number that was fifty points higher than the other families. They also controlled the numbers in the black neighborhoods. One day, Tumac was told to meet Giuseppe Abate on the Garden State Parkway and to give him his tribute from the numbers business, which was in a paper bag. Tumac was excited and honored that he was to meet the "Boss." When Abate arrived in his Chrysler, Tumac got in and they drove off. Tumac, in an attempt to ingratiate himself with the Boss, introduced himself by saying, "Hi Mr. Abate, I'm Anthony Accetturo. It's a pleasure to finally meet you." Guiseppe Abate stopped his car and ordered Tumac out. Tumac walked back to his car and, when he reported back to the Pizzolatos, he thought he was going to get whacked. He broke one of their rules by talking to the Boss. He learned a big lesson that day.

Chapter Sixteen

OC Committee

Also In 1963, United States Senator John Little McClellan (Dem. Arkansas) headed a committee on Organized Crime. They became known as the McClellan Hearings. The key witness was the infamous Joseph Valachi, a Genovese crime family soldier who was serving a life sentence for killing another inmate while serving time for murder. Valachi was the first Cosa Nostra turncoat who broke the silence of omerta. Valachi testified to the existence of the Cosa Nostra and identified the family structure and identified many of its members. It was the first time law enforcement received the intelligence that there was a national syndicate called the Cosa Nostra. They also learned that illicit gambling was the primary source of their income. Federal and state law enforcement agencies started to develop intelligence units and tactical organized crime units, mostly targeting gambling operations, which was considered the blood of the Cosa Nostra. The theory was that if government was to remove the Cosa Nostra's primary source of income, their organization would crumble. This was not completely true. They failed to give credit to Charles "Lucky" Luciano's mission statement when he orchestrated the creation of the American Mafia and the establishment of individual families in the early nineteen thirties. "We will create an organization that will change with the times and be everlasting." The Cosa Nostra has done just that. They have shown their resiliency and made adjustments and changes throughout the years.

PHOTO - TUMAC WITH MICHAEL AND MARTY TACCETTA

Daniel (Bobo) Ricciardi, left; Thomas Ricciardi, center, and William Corea, right, are escorted by FBI agents to appearances in the federal courthouse in Newark. The three Lucchese crime family members, some relatives and even their pets have been recommended for entry into the witness security program

PHOTO - TOMMY RICCIARDI AND WILLIAM COREA

PHOTO - MICHAEL TACCETTA

PHOTO - MARTY TACCETTA

Chapter Seventeen

The Taccetta's

Anthony "Tumac" Accetturo moved to Florida, where he started building an empire in that state. Florida has always been an open state for organized crime. Trafficante was the Boss of the only Florida-based Cosa Nostra family, but the only city he claimed as being exclusively under his control was Tampa. The other families were allowed to carry out their business in the state as long as he received their respect and they paid the proper tribute to him. Bingo on the Indian Reservations was an excellent source of income for the Indians. Tumac, recognizing the potential for income for his family, infiltrated that industry. Many of the reservations he shared with the Chicago syndicate and the mob from Pittsburgh. Tumac developed Cosa Nostra relationships with families across the nation. Tumac was a real politician. Tumac took care of the aging Boss of the Lucchese crime family, Ducks Carallo, and was on the move to someday become the Boss of the Lucchese family. He would occasionally host mob figures from across the country at the Diplomat Hotel in Hollywood Florida. Tumac started spreading his illicit operations across the country. Angelo Taccetta, a respected made guy from New Jersey, and his two sons, Michael and Marty, joined Tumac in Florida. Operating out of the Marco Polo Lounge in Hollywood, they started to become respected, and eventually they were sponsored by Tumac and became "made" in the Lucchese crime family. They returned to New Jersey to head the operations there. I always liked Michael and Marty. Michael had gone to school with my sister Patty at Our Lady of Valley School in Orange, and he always showed me respect. We had numerous conversations, and I liked, not what he stood for, but the way he always seemed to readily accept the fact that I would arrest him without hesitation and that he would have no problems with me. It was like a game. He was the bad guy and I was the good guy, and it was my job to catch him, and he expected it to happen, and that was the price of the business he had chosen. We had a conversation once in the hallway of the Essex County Courthouse where I was testifying on another matter. One of his guys was on trial for bookmaking in another courtroom. Michael said to me, "Could you imagine, one of my friends is on trial for bookmaking and the prosecutor has offered him three years if he pleads guilty?" He was crying the blues to me. He'd been a bookie for over thirty years without getting caught.

I asked him, "Thirty years ago, if the law came to you and offered you thirty years of amnesty as a bookmaker in return for three years in jail, would you have taken it?" He was quiet. Of course he would have taken that offer. Michael was a thinker. Of course I knew that both Michael and Marty didn't like me, but they always handled themselves well in my presence. I had told them that I would never embarrass them in front of their family, and I never did. I explained my rules to them. If I had an arrest warrant for murder or narcotics, then I would take them out any way I could, but if I was serving a subpoena, conducting an interview, or had a warrant for a minor offense, I would call them to meet me so I wouldn't have to upset any wives or kids. They knew of my sense of pride for my heritage and that I was dedicated to eradicate the Cosa Nostra and the stigma it put upon Italian-Americans. They also knew that if I made a case against them, it would be the result of a fair investigation and it would be a strong evidential case and very hard to beat. Years later, that's just what I did.

In 1984, while I was assigned to investigate organized crime's influence in the boxing industry, Michael and Marty were subjects of the investigation. Carlos Deluiis, the owner of The Meeting Place Restaurant in Madison, New Jersey, who was also an associate of Michael and Marty Taccetta, had a financial interest in an upcoming middle-weight named Bobby Cycz. The SCI issued subpoenas for Carlos, and Michael, and Marty Taccetta as well as several other associates. I called Michael and told him that I wanted to meet him to give him the subpoena. I asked him if he could bring his brother, Carlos, and the others named in the subpoenas. We arranged to meet at The Meeting Place. The Meeting Place was an excellent restaurant, but I never ate there for obvious reasons. I don't like the flavor of spit in my food. Many mob guys, including Sam "the Plumber" DeCavalcante, the head of the New Jersey Cosa Nostra family, frequented the restaurant. When I arrived, Michael and Marty were sitting at a table in the back and motioned for me to come to them. Prior to entering the restaurant, I saw a couple of his men sitting in a car in the parking lot. It was obvious that they were checking me out. When I approached Michael and Marty, I told them that they didn't have to have someone outside and that I was alone and only there to serve the subpoenas like I told him I would. In his rough voice, Michael told me that I was wrong, that he would never do anything like that. Yeah, right. He then asked me if I wanted something to eat, and I refused. I told him that I would like to serve the subpoenas, so he called Carlos over first. Poor Carlos, he was scared to death. He wasn't a bad guy, really. I arrested some of his family members a year or so before for bookmaking. Carlos was a gambler and blew a lot of money, which eventually caused him to lose his restaurant. It was a shame, because he was very likable and had a good business. He could have it made if he didn't get involved with the bad guys. After I served all of the subpoenas, I saw Brescia the Plumber, one of the boys, approach the table. He had a brown bag in his hand. Michael told me that he was extremely appreciative that I extended him the courtesy of not serving him in front of his family, and he had two bottles of wine that he knew I would love. I asked Michael if he was kidding. He should know that I wouldn't accept a gift from him. Marty got all nervous, looked at Michael, and said, "I told you not to offer him anything, now he thinks we're trying to bribe him." I said, "Relax, I'm not going to arrest you. I'll tell you what I'll do. Open it and I'll have a glass with you, as long as I pay."

Michael said, "It's on the house, but if that's the only way you'll taste the wine, it's a deal." He opened the wine. I put twenty dollars on the table and had a glass of wine.

I credit my success in law enforcement with my ability to get information from various sources. When I retired from the state police, I had over fifty registered informants. My theory was that you never knew what problems an individual had, especially with wise guys. They may have violated a Mafia rule and believed that they were going to be whacked, or they may have been pissed that they hadn't been promoted. I made it a practice of having a chat whenever I came in contact with a wise guy. If they decided to cooperate when they were faced with a problem, they were going to contact the law enforcement officer they knew and trusted.

Well, we had a couple of glasses of wine and I had the feeling that they were trying to get me drunk, but they didn't know that I could put both of them under the table when it came to drinking. Besides, I faked drinking most of the wine. Actually, we talked about the old times growing up in Orange. He told me that he had a big crush on my kid sister, and we talked about her. She was having some problems at the time with her husband. Michael seemed very concerned and asked, "Do you want me to handle him?" He added, "It would be a pleasure. I could make him a mushroom or just lay him on top of a mushroom." I got that message quickly. I told him that I could take care of my own family's problems, but thanks for the thought. Then he told me a story that is one of my all-time favorites. He told me that he knew how cops interpret conversations they intercept while conducting a wiretap. He gave me an example of how he could get in trouble for a misinterpretation of what was said. In his rough voice he said that he stopped over one of his guys' house and admired a lamp that he had. Randy, his friend, told Michael that he could get him one. A couple of days later Randy called Michael at his home phone and said, "Michael, I got that thing for you." Michael replied, "Don't say anything on the phone." Randy repeated several times that he got the thing for Michael. Michael demanded that Randy say that the thing was a lamp. Michael said to me, "Imagine. He called me up at my home and said he got that thing for me. If the feds or you guys were listening, I would have been indicted for drugs, right?"

I said, "That is one thing you should never say on the phone, the word 'thing'." Well, I learned something from that conversation. The word "thing" doesn't necessarily mean narcotics.

Years later my team would arrest Tumac, Michael, and Marty for racketeering, and they would all serve long terms in state prison.

The Lucchese crime family's associate, Vincent "Sinatra" Craparotta, wasn't sending the proper tribute to Michael and Marty Taccetta. Sinatra had registered SMS Vending Company with the Mob but had told the Taccettas that he wasn't earning from that company. The Taccettas sent him a message by beating him to death with a nine iron on June 12, 1984. Years later, we solved that murder and convicted the hierarchy of the New Jersey Lucchese crime family.

In December of 1985, the Boss of the Gambino crime family, Paul "Big Paulie" Castellano and his Underboss, Thomas Bilotti, were gunned down at the direction of John "Dapper Don" Gotti. Gotti then took over the reins of the Gambino crime family. Gotti's Neapolitan flamboyant style lead to the considerable weakening of that family's influence. One of his soldiers that he had elevated to Caporegime became Underboss.

The murder of Otto Patrick Marrone on August 24, 1980 personally bothered me because I knew Pat Marrone. I had met him through a very good friend of mine, Sal Apuzzio. Sal was a detective in the Union County prosecutor's office who later retired as a captain. Pat Marrone was a major earner for Anthony "Tumac" Accetturo and the Taccetta brothers, Michael and Marty. He had a garage on Route 22, a trucking company, and his own airplane.

On October 20, 1993, the New Jersey faction of the Lucchese crime family was found guilty of twenty years' worth of racketeering and engaging in murder in furtherance of the racketeering. Anthony Accetturo, Michael Taccetta, Marty Taccetta, and Thomas Ricciardi were convicted of racketeering and the 1984 murder of Vincent Craparotta, who refused to pay tribute to the Lucchese New Jersey faction. Facing thirty years in state prison, Anthony Acetturo and Thomas Ricciardi agreed to cooperate. Michael and Marty Taccetta and Michael Perna pled guilty to federal charges of corruption of Newark officials, extortion, and eleven gangland homicides. These convictions were the end of a twenty-year reign of terror by the Lucchese crime family in New Jersey. As I write this book, the defendants are being released from prison, and we will have to wait and see if they continue the life of a wise guy.

PHOTO - JACKIE DI NORSICIA

PHOTO - BUCKY JONES

PHOTO - GERRY CATENA

PHOTO - ANGELO BRUNO

Tino Fiumara

PHOTO - TINO FIUMARA

Michael Coppola, allegedly a major
player in the Genovese crime family.

PHOTO - MICHAEL COPPOLA, ALLEGEDLY A MAJOR PLAYER IN
THE GENOVESE CRIME FAMILY

BOIARDO ESTATE

Chapter Eighteen

Jackie Adams

Giacomo "Jackie Adams" DiNorscia was a rising star in the early eighties. I first heard about him when I read a report about an assault of an off-duty trooper at a nightclub down the Jersey Shore. It was a brutal beating, and Jackie was arrested. That assault on a trooper was probably the worst mistake Jackie ever made. He got my attention. I started checking him out and learned that he got his button (became made in the Cosa Nostra) when he gunned down a man who informed on Jackie's father Thomas "Tommy Adams" DiNorscia, a made man in the Bruno crime family. The man had testified against Tommy Adams and was given a one-way ticket out of Newark by the police. He made the mistake of returning to Newark, and Jackie killed him. Jackie was given Morris County to organize the independent bookmakers and develop the county for the Cosa Nostra. The state police received court authorization to wiretap several phones and interrupted the Cosa Nostra's plan. I personally went to arrest Jackie at his home in Nutley. Jackie was married and had two beautiful kids. We had a four-trooper arrest team and arrived in one car. I told the team that I would go to the door first and act as if I was a friend to find out if he was home. If he came to the door, I would simply place him under arrest. In my whole career, I was always concerned about the impact an arrest of a father would make on his children, so I would always attempt to make the arrest without the showing of guns or acting like the Gestapo. Jackie's wife came to the door and immediately invited me in, thinking that I was just a friend stopping by. When I entered,

I gave a signal to the rest of the team to follow me in. I asked where Jackie was and she told me he was upstairs. I immediately went up the stairs and followed the sound of a Looney Tunes cartoon from a television set. There he was in his bedroom lying on his bed in his boxer shorts, watching cartoons. The first thing he said was, "I should have known I was getting pinched when I heard four car doors slam shut." I instructed him that if he behaved, I wouldn't cuff him in front of his family and we would simply walk out of the house and I would cuff him outside. Jackie asked me if he could first take his medication, and I told him he could. There was a prescription bottle of Valium on his dresser, and he downed about a half dozen in one gulp and got dressed. Jackie sat in the middle of two troopers in the back seat and we took off to the Morris County Jail via the local streets. I told Jackie that he should never have assaulted the trooper, because that incident is what brought him to my attention. As we passed through a wooded rural area en route to the jail, Jackie became visibly upset. I asked him what the problem was and he said, "This is it, right? You are going to kill me." I told him to relax. When we got to the jail, Jackie extended his hand to me and thanked me for changing my mind and not killing him. Jackie received a five-year sentence, was caught bookmaking from prison, and received an extended sentence.

When he got out he was indicted again for racketeering, was found innocent, went into the drug business, got caught, and went back to jail, and he eventually died.

Jackie was a likeable guy and could have been a successful stand-up comedian. While on trial for racketeering in federal court in Newark he even had the judge laughing. Jackie acted as his own attorney. Jackie's antics in the courtroom had the jurors laughing, and to many who witnessed the trial, Jackie helped the defense team enormously in obtaining an acquittal. When asked by the court if he ever had any special training in the law, Jackie replied, "Judge, I've been in jail all my life." While on cross examination, the court was full of FBI agents. Jackie was asked if he was paranoid and thought there was an FBI agent behind every bush, and Jackie responded by looking around the courtroom and asking, "Was I wrong?"

His cross examination of the government's star witness, Jackie's cousin, Joseph Alonzo, although humorous, was very effective. Alonzo had shot Jackie several times and began to cooperate because he was in fear of retaliation by Jackie. Jackie fumbled his notes and messed around but also did a number on Alonzo. It was obvious that the jury liked Jackie more than Alonzo. Anyway, the entire New Jersey Lucchese crime family faction was tried and acquitted. They celebrated and had their moment of glory but later were not so lucky when our state task force successfully prosecuted the entire family hierarchy.

Jackie was a rising star and could have been a Boss, but he was the most unlucky mob guy I've ever dealt with. Part of his crew was Michael and Marty Taccetta and Bucky Jones. Jackie's godfather was Louie Luciano, a made guy in the Bruno crime family. Louie was having an affair with the wife of one of the Campisis and paid the ultimate price. He was murdered in front of his home in Roseland. I was assigned to cover the wake. Instead of sitting in a car taking plate numbers, I would stand with the other visitors. This worked for me since I am Italian and could certainly pass for a wise guy. I found I could mingle and most people would not take me for a cop. Jackie and his family arrived in a limo. He saw me and walked right over to me and re-introduced me to his wife. While we were talking, one of Jackie's guys came over. Jackie immediately introduced me and emphasized, "A detective with the state police."

The guy said, "Nice to meet you," then immediately turned to Jackie and said, "Jackie, the truck is in, what should we do?"

Jackie repeated, "Didn't you hear me?" "This is Bob Buccino, a state police detective." The guy said, "I heard you. Now what do you want me to do with the truck?"

Jackie turned to me and said, "Now you know why I always get pinched." He was a funny guy.

Chapter Nineteen

Illegal Casinos

Illegal casinos were throughout Hudson, Passaic, Essex, and Bergen counties. They were protected operations and were very profitable. I went undercover in East Newark and Harrison, where there were two gambling halls. One was a blackjack game, and the high rollers would be lugged to the second gambling hall where they gambled at monte. We hit these games several times in two years. The first time I played drunk and pretended to be asleep in a parked car directly across the road in an all-night diner's parking lot. From this surveillance point, I was able to identify their signal for admittance and estimate the number of allowed participants. I worked alone in those days with no backup and no communications. If something happened to me, my office wouldn't know about it until they read it in the papers. One night, as I played drunk and sleeping, a group of men came out of the gambling hall, crossed the street, and were bullshitting and leaning on my car. One of them slammed his hand on the roof of my care directly above my head. I almost had a heart attack, but I didn't move. There was laughter, and they soon left and went back to the gambling hall. When they were out of sight, I went into the diner. For some reason I had to go to the bathroom. A couple of days later, I walked right past the lookout man, gave a signal, and walked into the game. I was wearing a black trench coat. After I observed the men who were operating the games, I walked out the front door, which was the signal for the troopers to raid the game. When the troopers entered, they immediately photographed the entire room and lined all the prisoners against a wall to begin processing them. So there were all the participants in the game against one wall and all the cops lined up facing them. I noticed that there were three made guys missing from the group lined against the wall. I knew they were there before. I mentioned it to a detective standing by my side, but when I didn't like the way he responded I looked at him and it was one of the wise guys. When we entered the room, the three made guys had slipped over to the side with the troopers and started giving commands like they were detectives. I corrected that immediately. One of the wise guys gave me some good advice. He told me that when I walked in looking the way I did with a black trench coat, they thought I was going to rob the place. They were getting ready to give me a beating. He suggested that the next time I do it, I should shout out, "state police!" to prevent a terrible mistake from happening. We made sixty arrests that day. We hit that game about five times in two years. Every time we hit it, they changed their security. The first time we hit it we simply walked in. The second time, we had to use battery rams to break through the bolted door. The third time, they had installed a steel door, but we were still able to ram it open. The fourth time, they installed a steel door filled with cement with steel jams, and the door opened outward. We had a hard time getting in. Wait until you hear about the fifth time we hit.

Once again, I played drunk and identified the location where the monte game was. I sat on a curb playing as if I were a drunk, and every hour on the hour a limo would arrive bringing the high rollers. Just before the limo would arrive, a police cruiser would arrive. When the limo stopped in front of the gambling hall, the police lieutenant would approach the driver and get an envelope. I was able to observe that they had a six-by-eight beam latched across the door to prevent us from ramming the door open. I had an idea. We would use chainsaws. The night of the raid, we put the entire raiding team in the back of a van with the chainsaws running. When we hit the door, it made a racket, and it still took a long time to get inside, but when we did, we couldn't believe our eyes. The players were frozen at the tables still with the cards and money in front of them. There were several men under the tables, and the place stunk. Several men shit their pants and several others pissed themselves. Apparently, we made quite an entrance. This made the processing quite difficult, because we had to put up with the stench of human waste. When we got inside, we called the local police. Guess who arrived with them? The lieutenant who received the envelopes. When he entered, he started shouting at the prisoners, "You punks, I told you to stay out of my town. We run a clean town here." I walked over to the lieutenant and whispered in his ear, "We had this place under surveillance for a couple of weeks." He looked at me and quietly offered me any assistance I needed. I was burned out working undercover on these games. I brought in a young trooper who grew up in Hudson County. We got the trooper in the monte game and later raided the game, arresting over fifty participants. When the trial came up, the trooper testified, describing the game of monte and his undercover role. On cross-examination, the defense attorney asked the trooper where he learned how to play monte, and the trooper took the fifth. I couldn't believe my ears. He thought he had committed a crime by learning the game on the streets of Hudson County while he was growing up.

It could only happen in Hudson County. One time I was testifying and under direct by an assistant prosecutor. There were two assistant prosecutors at the prosecution table. When the A.P. examining me asked a question that was critical to my testimony, the other A.P. stood up and shouted, "I object!" Another time, while querying the potential jurors, the question was asked, "What are your feelings about bookmakers?" An elderly woman responded, "They are OK, as long as they pay up on time."

Chapter Twenty

Structure of the OC

Structure of New Jersey's Mob during the sixties and seventies:
There were seven Cosa Nostra families operating in the State of New Jersey. The most powerful was the Genovese crime family, named after Vito Genovese from the Highlands. Philip "Cockeyed Phil" Lombardo of Bergen County and Alphonso "Funzi" Tieri of Fort Lee were the acting Bosses after Vito was incarcerated for a narcotics conviction. Gerry Catena of West Orange, New Jersey was the consigliore along with Giuseppe "Pepe" Sabata of Bergen County. Their trusted Capo regimes were Ruggeri "the Boot" Boiardo of Livingston, New Jersey. Angelo "Gyp" DeCarlo of Mountainside, Anthony "Tony Pro" Provenzano of the Teamsters and Bergen County, and Peter "The Nose" LaPlaca of Lodi. Their trusted soldiers were Andy Gerardo, John "Big Pussy" Russo, Anthony "Little Pussy" Russo, Angelo Sica, Emilio "The Count" DeLio, Anthony Devingo, Vincent "Jimo" Calabrese, Tobias Boyd, Dan "Red" Cecere, Nunzio Sica, Tino "Handsome Harry" Fiumaro, Louis "Streaky" Gatto, Michael Coppola, Peter Greco, John DiGilio, Ernest Palmieri, Louis "Bobby" Manna, Thomas "Timmy Murphy" Pecora, and Peter Polidori. There were over twenty members of the Genovese crime family operating in the State of New Jersey in the early seventies. They influenced the garbage, vending, construction, trucking, and seaport industries in the state.

The Gambino family was named after Carlo Gambino. "The Boss of Bosses" was very powerful in the State of New Jersey. Carlo was the Boss in the seventies, and his trusted Caporegime in New Jersey was Joseph Paterno of Newark. Little Puss Russo, a soldier in the Genovese family, who was Vito Genovese's driver and bodyguard, lived in Long Branch. While incarcerated, Little Pussy made comments that he was going to kill the trooper who arrested him.

When I heard about this, another trooper and I paid a visit to his Boss, Joe Paterno, at his home in Newark. Paterno had a maid, and his wife was not an Italian. We were invited into his dining room where we were served pastry and coffee. Joe Paterno engaged us in small talk, actually telling us how much he respected the New Jersey state police and how it was a shame about the crime in his neighborhood. When we told him about the comments that Little Pussy Russo was making from prison about killing the arresting trooper, he said that the state police should not concern ourselves with the comments because Little Pussy had a big mouth and didn't mean what he said. Paterno assured us that nothing would ever happen to the trooper. We knew right away that Pussy Russo would get the message loud and clear from Joe Paterno.

Angelo "Gyp" DeCarlo, a Genovese crime family Caporegime, was one of the most significant mobsters in North Jersey. His headquarters was in Mountainside, but most of his crew was in the Orange area and led by his most trusted soldier, Dan "Red" Cecere. Gyp was a sadistic and brutal man, but if you saw him you would think he was someone's gentle uncle. He wasn't flamboyant like John Gotti. He was just one of the guys. He didn't want to be known as a racketeer but liked to be known as an old gangster. Bookmaking and loan sharking were his primary criminal activities. His family also had influence with the Teamsters and the Laborers and had interests in Las Vegas and a casino in Antigua. I met him a couple of times in the sixties at the Berkeley Bar on Essex Avenue in Orange. In those days, he answered directly to Gerry Catena, the then acting Boss of the Genovese family. He made his button with the Cosa Nostra when he was part of the hit squad that wacked Dutch Schultz. Daniel "Red" Cecere was a soldier under DeCarlo and made Orange his headquarters. If he wasn't at the Berkeley, he would be at his barn in Mountainside. The FBI had bugged the Mountainside barn, and when they released the tapes, the Cosa Nostra in Essex County was finally revealed. DeCarlo did a lot of talking and the feds did a lot of listening. One of his soldiers was Lenny Macaluso. I knew Lenny and liked him a lot. We used to hang at Schimele's Pool Hall and shot a lot of pool together. If I didn't get married, I am certain I would have been right alongside Lenny. Lenny was running Gyp's bookmaking and doing strong-arm work for him. I gave Lenny several breaks without him even knowing it. I never targeted him, but if I wanted to, he would have been easy, since I knew everyone he was with. DeCarlo was convicted of extortion in 1970 and sentenced to twelve years in prison. He was pardoned by President Nixon after two years. I wonder who he knew. He was close to several politicians like Congressman Peter Rodino and then-Mayor Hugh Addonizio. He died in 1973.

In the late fifties and early sixties, he had a contract with Jimmy Roselle, a popular singer from Hoboken. Jimmy Roselle, who many people felt was as good as or if not better than Frank Sinatra, would not play ball with the mob. He knew that they would eventually own him, so he broke away from DeCarlo. Roselle was black-balled by the industry and couldn't even get his records played on the radio. In 1969, when Gyp was arrested for extortion and the Saperstein murder, one of the detectives had to use his bathroom, and when he lifted the seat to take a piss, there was a photograph of Jimmy Roselle in the bowl. Gyp would piss on him every day. I knew all the members of his crew, so I decided to target his operation. One of the methods I used in those days was that I would steal their garbage in the early morning hours. One morning, about 3:00 a.m., I went to Cecere's house in West Orange. The garbage cans were by the back of the house under a set of windows. As I was looking through the garbage, I made some noise. The window opened right above me and it was Red Cecere. I squirreled myself against the wall and started doing my best impersonation of a cat. "Meow, meow." He cursed the cat and closed the window. I got out of there as fast as I could. I began intense surveillances and developed probable cause to obtain search warrants for over ten locations when the FBI publicly disclosed the fact that they had an illegal bug in Gyp DeCarlo's Mountainside headquarters and they released all the transcripts in federal court. In the transcripts there were conversations about the state police, and there was reference to Colonel David B. Kelly, the superintendent. They referred to the colonel as a good guy, and in another conversation they talked about a Kelly, but the media publicized the conversations about Colonel Kelly. Colonel Kelly was a man of high integrity, and he proved it by his actions against organized crime and corruption. He was my idol. New Jersey had the reputation of being corrupt state controlled by organized crime. By the way, that reputation was warranted. Colonel Kelly was so upset that he had a heart attack. While in the hospital, he ordered his Deputy Superintendent Eugene Olaffto to target Gyp DeCarlo, and he declared war against the Cosa Nostra. When Olaf returned to headquarters he called for a meeting with his newly created Intelligence Bureau and Organized Crime Bureau. Unfortunately, there was little intelligence on Gyp DeCarlo's operation. An intelligence officer, Detective Bill Turner, was familiar with my work and brought it up at the meeting. I was called into Trenton and temporarily assigned to the elite Intelligence Bureau. A task force was created, and the first operation by the taskforce was called "Operation Godfather". I don't know how they thought of that name; probably a high-ranking officer, probably a major. When I went to my new assignment, I had built up my squad to a four-member unit, and we had arrested over two hundred associates of organized crime for various illegal gaming offenses. I was very successful and was developing a good reputation among law enforcement. I was and still am very proud of my heritage, and I wanted desperately to rid Italian Americans of this cancer called the Cosa Nostra. I was on a mission. I had a knack for developing informants. Whenever I arrested a bookmaker, I would give them an offer they couldn't refuse. I offered them a recommendation for a non-custodial sentence if they could provide me information that led to the arrests of three bookmakers of equal or higher-up rank than he was. At one time, in my early years, I had fifty-eight informants registered with the state police. Our task force was very successful. We were arresting bookmakers and number operatives every week. Of course, they were all credited to "Operation Godfather". Legislation was passed in New Jersey that allowed law enforcement to wiretap those suspected of crimes related to organized crime. Colonel Kelly also hired two young attorneys, Ed Stier and Pete Richards. Ed and Pete were aggressive attorneys with the United States Attorney's Office in Newark. They were assigned directly to the Intelligence Bureau. They brought with them Bob Jordan from the United States Marshall Service to act as their investigator. Years later they would break off from the state police and become the New Jersey Division of Criminal Justice. I had a wonderful and close relationship through the years with all three of them.

RICHIE THE BOOT BOIARDO
Ruggerio "Richie the Boot" Boiardo was the most respected and influential mob guy in New Jersey. Richie was the real "Godfather." He was born in Naples December 8, 1890. He was an orphan and moved to the United States

with his adopted parents in 1901. He settled in Newark in 1906 and married Jennie Manfro in 1912. He did time for running a gambling house, manslaughter, and carrying a concealed weapon. He served a little over a year on all charges. In 1920, during prohibition, the Boot ran gambling houses and speakeasies throughout New Jersey. It was during this time that a nexus developed between politicians, police officers, and celebrities who visited his illegal operations. It was said that the Boot had all the politicians and cops in his back pocket. He, once again, did time for weapons possession and returned to Newark in 1933. Prohibition was appealed. Lucky Luciano, the new Boss, had orchestrated the murder of Joe "the Boss" Masseria and Salvatore Maranzano, the Bosses of the two Mafia families. It was said that the Boot was one of the gunmen in that Mafia war. Lucky Luciano brought into Atlantic City all the Bosses nationally. He established guidelines and rules governing the newly created American Mafia, along with territorial boundaries. He created a national commission and an East Coast commission. He created five New York families, one New Jersey family, and one Philadelphia family. The Boot was a soldier under Lucky Luciano. Luciano and was followed by Frank Costello and then by Vito Genovese. In the '50s, the mob and the Boot flourished. They were making tons of money from their gambling, loansharking, and labor racketeering. The Boot had a great advantage. He wasn't being bothered, because of his connections with politicians and cops. When Genovese became Boss, he promoted the Boot to Caporegime. In New Jersey, the Silver Lake section of Belleville that bordered Newark had the most mob crews. All five families were represented in this small area. The most powerful were the Gambino family, headed by Capo Joseph Paterno, and the Genovese family, headed by Richie "the Boot" Boiardo. Both men had different management styles.

Boiardo's crews ran the numbers and sports betting operations. He worked closely with the other families and the other Capos in the Genovese family, such as Tony Pro Provenzano and Gyp DeCarlo. He had strong influence over several unions, such as the Ironworkers, the Teamsters, and the Laborers. His crews made a lot of money. It wasn't all peaches and cream. Occasionally there would be a dispute between the families, and a bullet-ridden body would show up on the avenue.

He had a financial interest in the casinos in Vegas, the Caribbean, Antigua, and Atlantic City. Angelo Chieppa, his trusted lieutenant and closest friend, ran the Casino in Antigua, was suspected of skimming, and was found in the trunk of a car. There was only one person who could have sanctioned that "hit," and that was "the Boot." The message was "You don't steal from a Boss. No matter who you are." The fact of the matter was, the Casino wasn't making money. All the freeloaders from Essex County invaded the Casino and cheated the games. It wasn't Chieppa skimming; he just couldn't stop the leaks.

Nineteen fifty-seven was an interesting year for the Cosa Nostra. First, the Sicilian Mafia brought in heroin. The Bureau of Narcotics (DEA) rounded up hundreds of Mafioso and had them deported. Joseph Bonnanno, representing the American Mafia, went to Sicily and met with the Bosses of the Sicilian Mafia. It was at this meeting in the Hotel dePalms that the American Mafia broke away from their Sicilian cousins. Joseph Bonnanno told his Sicilian cousins that the Americans would no longer deal in Narcotics. They would, however, assist when needed. They were given the franchise to transport and distribute drugs in the USA as long as their business did not interfere with the American businesses. The Americans would disallow any attacks on police officers or prosecutors, an attack the Sicilians did frequently. Joseph Bonnanno knew that the Americans had their gambling, labor unions, extortion racket, loansharking, etc. Drugs were a dirty business and would result in the demise of the Mafia.

When Joseph Bonnanno returned, there was a meeting at Ruggerio Boiardo's house in Livingston. The meeting was attended by the five New York families and the New Jersey and Philadelphia families. The new rules were accepted by all, and the punishment for violating these rules would be death. The Cosa Nostra ("this thing of ours") was born. This meeting was the prelude to the infamous meeting at Apalachin, New York, where the Bosses of twenty-eight mob families met over the new rules governing the Cosa Nostra. Boiardo demanded compliance by his entire crew. Of course there were some who were involved in the drug business, but they acted alone and never used the Boiardo name or influence to conduct their business. I am certain that when they brought cash to Boiardo, he didn't reject any money that he suspected of being the proceeds of a drug transaction.

In 1970, the Boot began a prison sentence for running a gambling operation. He was serving time in the New Jersey State Prison and I was assigned to intelligence in the state police. I receive a letter with a drawing of a swimming pool. It was from the Boot who requested consideration to build a swimming pool for the inmates at his expense. Was he kidding? Who knows.

I felt it was humorous. I decided to visited him in prison and personally tell him the bad news of rejection. When I went to see him I was told by the warden that I would be escorted by a corrections officer to meet with Boiardo. As we waked across the yard, I noticed a beautiful tomato garden. I walked over to it to get a better look when I was warned not to touch the "Old man's tomatoes." No, the Old Man was not the warden; it was Boiardo's garden. Amazing. Anyway, I had a great conversation with the Boot. Most of the conversation was about his younger days. He seemed open about the bootlegging days and the celebrities he knew. He loved talking about food and Bloomfield Avenue. I enjoyed talking to him. It was like talking to my grandfather. Anyway, he didn't serve much time, and when he was release I stuck with him like glue. I would sit in front of his driveway on Beuford Place in Livingston facing north. Every day he would drive himself in his old Plymouth out of the driveway make a right turn and stop at Capone's Gulf Station and hang out for a while before he would drive down Bloomfield Avenue to Newark. One day he made a left turn from his driveway instead of a right, crossing me up. He passed me and I had to make a U-turn. When I faced the direction he was traveling in, I noticed that he had stopped on the shoulder. He waived at me and signaled me to follow him. He was playing with me.

On November 17, 1984, at the age of ninety-three, the Boot passed away. It was very easy to identify all of Boot's soldiers, because when they became "made," the Boot presented them with a statue to put on their front lawn. I knew the Boot had died because when I drove passed his soldier, Anthony DeVingo's house on Passaic Avenue, I saw him removing the statue. His whole crew removed their statues the same day.

In the early '80s a detective, "Dennis," who worked for me in the state police asked to see me and said that it was very important. It was a Friday and he came into my office and reported to me that he was offered a bribe by a state police sergeant. I told him to go home and think of what he was about to tell me; to submit to me his allegations in writing and that I would handle it. There would be no cover-up. On Monday I received his report, and I asked him to come and see me so I could have all the facts. As a result, I had the following facts: Dennis was moonlighting as a bouncer at a club in Ortley Beach, New Jersey when a fight broke out inside the club. In breaking up the fight, one guy involved in the fight resisted and Dennis arrested him and charged him for being disorderly; a minor offense, but it turned out to be a major incident. Now, by telling me this, Dennis was admitting that he violated state police procedure for moonlighting. What was interesting was that the guy he arrested was Phil Lombardi, Jr., the son of the Boss of the Genovese crime family. The owner of the club, Joey B., was an ex-boxer and a guy who was close to a lot of mob guys. Phil Lombardi, Sr. was pissed off because Joey B. allowed his son to get arrested in his club and wanted it "Taken care of." Joey B. had a cousin in the state police who was a sergeant and actually lived in an apartment above the club. The sergeant "Joey L." was well liked in the state police, and at the request of Joey B. he approached Dennis in an attempt to have the disorderly person charge dismissed. Dennis refused even after being promised money. That is when Dennis came to me and reported the incident. Now, I know you noticed that I am not using their names. That is because we are talking about an incident that happened more than thirty years ago, and Dennis has since passed away, and the others have paid for what they have done, so I felt in all fairness that I would not mention some names.

I ordered Dennis to wear a wire and meet with Joey L. and discuss his bribe. It was successful, and we now had incriminating conversations with Joey L. I felt that the next course of action was to get Joey L.'s cooperation, so I called him into my office and confronted him with the evidence. He knew he just blew his job, so he decided to cooperate by also wearing a wire. After recording many incriminating conversations with several mob guys who were under Phil Lombardi, a sit-down was arranged. At the sit down was Streaky, a Genovese captain, Joey B., Joey L., and two prominent attorneys, Attorney Don C. who was President of the New Jersey Bar Association and Phil R., a powerful attorney from Bergen County. Anyway, they were all indicted except for Streaky, who did not utter one word at the meeting. All this for a disorderly person charge which probably would only have been a $100 fine.

The trial started in Ocean County Superior Court, and I was the main witness. Now, before this case, the words organized crime were not allowed in court. A police office could not even say that he/she was assigned to an Organized Crime Unit. Up till this case, the courts felt that it would be too prejudicial. Anyway, the two attorneys were high profile, and Don C. had as his attorney a popular attorney from South Jersey, Francis H. He was the lead attorney. On cross examination of me he asked several stupid questions. One question he asked was how I knew it was Phil Lombardi Jr. who was arrested rather that his father, since both had the same name. He was attempting to show that the only reason I would get involved in a small case was that I thought that the Lombardi arrested was significant person. My answer blew him away. I said that I happened to know that Phil Lombardi, Sr. had severe arthritis and was almost crippled. No way would he be going to disco. When the jury laughed, I knew I won that round, but the best was yet to come. As Francis H. was finishing his cross, he asked, I paraphrase, "By the way. Genovese, Genovese, what is this Genovese?" Genovese was in the report, but I never mentioned it because I knew I was not allowed to in court. But, since he opened the door, I gave a two hour lecture on the Genovese organized crime family. The other attorneys tried to stop me, but the court allowed me to continue. The other attorneys stipulated that I was a qualified expert on organized crime. Attorney Don C. was convicted. I felt bad about this because I never believed he was in any way affiliated with organized crime. I believe he was just invited to the meeting without knowing what it was about. Attorney Phil R. was acquitted. He had a great character witness, Peter Falk, Colombo fame, who was allowed to testify a lot more than a character witness usually is allowed. For example, Falk was able to come out with the fact that he knew that his friend was not involved because he (Falk) was the greatest detective in the world. I knew we were in trouble because during a break Jurors were lined up to get his autograph. All the defendants did their time, and I really don't know what happened to most of them. Joey B. continued to be a successful nightclub owner. Joey L. was relocated to the West Coast and I understand that he made a very good living building homes. Don C. could not practice law, but I heard he made a lot of money in real estate. I hope he did well, because it always bothered me that he was convicted. Dennis passed away several years ago. He had left the state police and went to work in Pennsylvania before he died.

Chapter Twenty-one

Atlantic City

When the State of New Jersey approved casino gambling in Atlantic City, they publicized that "New Jersey will keep the mob out of Atlantic City." What a joke. The mob was in Atlantic City before the casinos were even a thought. Atlantic City was an "open city" for the mob. The Lucchese crime family via Giuseppe Abate and the Bruno (Philadelphia) crime family via Nicky Scarfo controlled gambling, prostitution, and the labor unions way before the casinos opened. Antonio "Tony Bananas" Caponegro, a Bruno Caporegime who headed the North Jersey crew, felt that his Boss, Angelo Bruno, was too giving to the other families. He felt that the Bruno family should claim Atlantic City as its exclusive property. Caponegro was closely aligned to the New York families and believed that his association with the Genovese family, the most powerful of the New York families, would support him if he wanted to take over his family by murdering his Boss, Angelo Bruno. In March of 1980, Angelo Bruno was gunned down by a shotgun blast in his car on the streets of Philadelphia. Antonio Caponegro orchestrated the murder. Caponegro soon found out that he had broken a cardinal rule in the Cosa Nostra. He killed a Boss without the approval of the commission. John DiGilio, a soldier in the Genovese family from Bayonne, hated Caponegro. Several years before, there was a numbers man from Jersey City named Newsboy Moriarty who had died and left behind a lucrative numbers business. Both DiGilio and Caponegro claimed his numbers business. There was a sit-down and DiGilio lost out to Caponegro. DiGilio was hard-headed and an ex-boxer street-tough type and could not accept "losing" to Caponegro. One day, Caponegro and his brother-in-law were invited to the Genovese social club in lower Manhattan by Fat Tony Salerno on the pretense that the Genovese family would support his taking over of the Philadelphia family, but to his surprise, he was met instead by John DiGilio and his baseball bat. Caponegro was beaten to death and twenty dollar bills were shoved up his ass to give the message that he was killed because of his greed. The death of Bruno was the beginning of an internal war in Philadelphia that has left over forty made guys killed gangland style and the change of leadership over a half dozen times. While discussing the actions of the Philadelphia family, one mob guy told me that the Philadelphia family was the only army that killed its own soldiers. He said that the threat of killing was more effective than the actual killing. Anyway, the Philadelphia family still has most of the loan sharking and illegal gambling in Atlantic City. They also control the sale of methamphetamines through their close association with the motorcycle gangs. But the city is still an open city, and all the New York families have influence in the labor unions and many of the service industries. In recent years, there has been accepted competition from the Russian Mafia, especially in the pawn shops, go-go bars, strip clubs, and prostitution. There isn't anything you can't get in Atlantic City.

OPERATION PISCES

I was in charge of the Intelligence Bureau's North Unit when we conducted an undercover investigation in Atlantic City. The Staten Island Colombo family had developed a fraudulent scheme against the casinos. When a gambler would become indebted to one of their bookmakers in Staten Island, they would force him to commit fraud against the casinos and turn the money over to the mob in payment of his losses. Utilizing the mob's contacts in the casinos and in several banks, they would establish a credit line in one of the casinos. They would open a bank account with ten thousand dollars at a friendly bank. The gambler would apply for credit at one of the casinos and us the new bank account as a reference. The casinos had a policy that the bank account had to be at least nine months old to be accepted, but that's where the friendly

banker came in. When the casino would call the bank, they were told that the account was an old account and that there was ten thousand dollars in it. The casino would then give the gambler a credit line of up to ten thousand dollars. On a Friday night, mob guys like Frank Piccone and Vinnie Billelo would accompany several of the gamblers to the casinos, where they would draw the chips, go to the craps table, and, utilizing signals across the table, the mob guys would play the same amount but opposite the bet on the pass line. This would show the casinos that the player was gambling the money but in fact was just laundering the money across the table. They would play craps until the gambler would lose all his chips while across the table, and the wise guy would win the amount he lost. At the end of the evening, the mob guy would cash in the remaining chips and repay the gambler's debt, then leave the gambler a few bucks and a ten thousand-dollar debt to the casino. In some cases, they would then repay the original casino credit and increase the credit line to an amount as high as they could before they ripped it off. In some cases, it would be an amount in excess of fifty thousand dollars. Of course, the casinos were never paid and had to write off the loss. In those days, the Casino Control Commission allowed the casinos to write off about four percent of its losses, so the casinos didn't push too hard to collect small debts. I had two of my detectives, Billy Newsome and Nick Oriola, infiltrate their operation. They did a great job and actually began working in the role of the mob guys in washing the money across the craps table. We learned that they were exchanging the chips and money in their hotel room, so we obtained a court order to bug the room they were staying in. Of course we wouldn't know their room number in advance, so we obtained and bugged common hotel furniture. Once the mob guys registered and got a room, we would simply change their furniture with the bugged furniture when they were on the floor gambling. It was quite successful. Once we had their room bugged, we would get a room on the same floor as close as possible to their room so we could monitor and make observations. The court allowed us to monitor when they were in the room with whomever they met, including casino workers. We had to use headsets with our monitors because the walls were so thin and we didn't want any other hotel guests to hear anything.

Frankie P. was some man. During an evening, he would bring at least five cocktail waitresses to the room for sex. We would listen until the sex act began and then minimize our monitoring. Frankie enticed the cocktail waitresses by offering them cocaine. He would entice them by putting cocaine on his penis to get them to perform oral sex on him. On one occasion, one of my troopers who was monitoring by listening on the headset became visibly upset and starting shouting, "Oh no, oh no, I can't believe she's doing that!" I immediately asked him what was wrong and found out that Frankie P had just brought the trooper's girlfriend to the room and was having sex with her. What are the odds of that even happening? I asked the trooper about his relationship with the young lady and when he expected to see her again. He told me that he loved her, and that they were getting engaged and that he was going to meet her that morning when she got off work. I had to sit this guy down man to man. We had a long talk and I think he handled it well. He eventually married her. I guess he forgave her. We all make mistakes now and then. When we arrested Frankie and Vinnie, I asked Vinnie what he thought about Frankie's escapades, and Vinnie said, "Frankie is a nymphomaniac." The state police had just started an Atlantic City Special Investigations Unit and placed it under the leadership of Jack Carney, a good friend of mine and a super competent detective. Carney was a state police "company man." He was a polished officer and kept his office as if he was General McCarthy, cannons and all. Since this was the first case of its kind in Atlantic City, it was decided that they would take the case and my unit would turn all evidence and give them the arrests. Carney had a sergeant who worked for him named Sergeant Ski, who was his "does it all" right hand. One morning after a successful evening, we had arranged to meet with Carney and his sergeant at their office in Absecon where we would give them a briefing and turn over our evidence, which that day was casino chips and a small quantity of cocaine. Before our meeting, we stopped at a diner for some breakfast and thought we would have some fun with Sergeant Ski. I took some foil from a pack of cigarettes, put some sugar in it, and made a fold to simulate cocaine. When we stopped at Carney's office, I gave him a briefing and then took out the deck of cocaine (sugar). Carney snapped out an order to Sergeant Ski, "Sergeant, take possession of the cocaine." I proceeded in opening the deck, putting some on my finger, and tasting it as if I was checking the quality. As Carney and Ski's eyes widened, I began passing it around to my detectives so they too have a taste. When it came back to me, I intentionally spilled the remaining sugar on the carpet. Ski snapped to and rushed to get a vacuum cleaner, put in a new bag, and started vacuuming up the sugar. I then pulled from my pocket the real packet of cocaine to give to Ski. Carney caught on right away and started to laugh, but I think Ski still believes the sugar was cocaine.

It was a great job and we had a lot of fun while working it. The state gave me two thousand dollars a night to give to my detectives since they had to go to the tables and gamble so they wouldn't look suspicious. I thought one of my detectives, Lenny Marsh, was going to get sucked into a slot machine. Whenever I needed him, that was where he could be found, at the slot machines. One night he was missing for a while. When I found him and asked where he was, he told me he lost all the money except for ten dollars and then went to the boardwalk for a stroll when he ran into a pregnant Asian hooker. He said he gave her four dollars for some sex but saved six dollars so he could make a comeback on the slots. After a few minutes, I couldn't find him again, and when I did, I asked him where he went. This time he told me that he went looking for the hooker to borrow the four dollars back. What a piece of work he was. My good friend, Him Sweeney, was assigned to follow Vinnie and Frankie between the casinos and let us know when they were returning to Bally's Casino where my team was set up. Jim was about six foot five and hit the scale at about three hundred twenty pounds. I was getting impatient and decided to go on the boardwalk and see if I could find Sweeney and our targets. I couldn't believe what I saw. Jim had hired a rickshaw to cart his fat ass around while he was following Vinnie and Frankie. What a crew. Frankie and Vinnie both went to jail for several years and continued their organized crime careers when they got out. Frankie became made with the Colombo crime family and Vinnie worked with the Gambino crew. The state police continued Operation Pisces for several years and ended up arresting over fifty individuals, many of whom were casino employees. While working undercover in Atlantic City, there was nothing we couldn't get. We were offered comps for a bribe, sex, any kind of drugs, illegal gambling, stolen property, and whatever we needed. Upon conclusion of our assignment, I submitted a written recommendation to continue utilizing deep undercover detectives in the casinos, but my recommendation was ignored. I think the state didn't want to piss off the casinos.

Chapter Twenty-two

First Rico Case

The Division of Criminal Justice director, Bob Winter, and I met to review old cases and to discuss potential organized crime cases. Bob was an environment expert. He was instrumental in developing an anti-trust prosecution on numerous organized crime members and garbage men and was also a key initiator of the A-901 law that requires that a person or corporation subject themselves to a background investigation to obtain a license in order to operate a business in the garbage industry. His effort was quite successful in cleaning up the industry in New Jersey. Unfortunately, A-901 became a prejudicial and ethnic profiling instrument that derogated hardworking, decent Italian Americans in the industry. But that is another story. As Bob and I went through the cases, he brought out one case that there was a recommendation to close from CJ's Environmental Section. The case involved the extensive dumping of demolition waste from New York in North Bergen. I knew that Sam Gravano, at that time a Caporegime in the Gambino crime family, controlled the disposal of demolition and construction waste, and I also knew that nothing could be brought into North Bergen without the approval of Joseph Mocco, a North Bergen political leader who was suspected of being corrupt for many years. Many of the dump trucks identified as bringing material to North Bergen were also affiliated with organized crime. I took over the case. I still feel that this was one of our best efforts and one of the best cases we ever made. It was a case that had been destined for closure.

We conducted several wiretaps and numerous surveillances and successfully did so without the use of one informant. We targeted two Gambino associates, Michael Harvan and Richard Bassi. A break came in the case when we heard Harvan tell Bassi that he had the "loppy" for that evening. Bob Carroll, the chief attorney for the task force, was trying to decipher the meaning of the word "loppy," and I told him it was short for "envelope" and that there was going to be a payoff that evening. Our surveillance team documented Harvan and Bassi meeting with the deputy chief of police of North Bergen, Joseph Dulanie, and giving him an envelope. This case resulted in the execution of twenty-six search warrants in New Jersey and New York, the arrest and prosecution of sixteen members and associates of the Gambino crime family, the prosecution of six corporations, and the seizure of numerous dump trucks for charges including racketeering, tampering with public records, official misconduct, and conspiracy. Key figures prosecuted were Joseph Mocco, the North Bergen municipal clerk, Joseph Dulainie, the deputy chief of police, Eddie "Cousin Eddie" Garafola, a soldier in the Gambino crime family who was also the brother in law of Sam "Sammy the Bull" Gravano, George Hurtuk, the licensing official in North Bergen, Michael Harvan, and Richard Bassi. Soon after these arrests, Sammy the Bull murdered Ed Garafola, the Bull's brother in law. We probably could have gotten Sammy the Bull too, but that would have expanded our electronic surveillance into New York, and our superiors would not have agreed to that.

Richard Bassi was quite a lover. We had a tap on his phone and, one night after a telephone conversation, his phone was not put back on the cradle correctly and thus kept an open line. We were allowed to go in and out of the line, and if we believed the conversation to be pertinent to the case, we would continue to monitor and record. If it wasn't pertinent, we would disconnect. While the phone was off the cradle we heard his girlfriend barking and howling. They were a match made in heaven.

To show you just how enterprising the Cosa Nostra is, we developed intelligence on their plans to dispose of New York demolition waste. Sammy the Bull controlled the disposal of construction waste in New York. Matty "The Horse" Tamello, a Genovese Caporegime, controlled the garbage industry in New Jersey. Sammy and Matty went up to West Milford in northern New Jersey and looked at a quarry to purchase. Their plan was to excavate and then fill the crater with the demolition waste. They were always thinking. Later, Sam the Bull became the Underboss of the Gambino crime family under the infamous John Gotti, the Boss.

While Richard Bassi and Michael Harvan were awaiting trial, they moved their operation to Newark and started dumping under a major highway intersection on Route 1. We found out about it and tried to shut them down. We executed a search warrant and while on the property, Michael Harvan, who was operating a bulldozer, saw me and drove the bulldozer toward me as if he was going to run me over. I played John Wayne and stood tall in the middle of the lane. As he approached me, I drew my weapon and pointed it directly at him. He stopped. I walked over to the cab of the bulldozer and pulled him off the seat. I threw him against a fence, slammed him a couple of times, and cuffed him. He apologized and told me his life story, so I didn't charge him with the threat. We went into court, but we got a liberal judge who allowed them to keep the illegal dumpsite operating.

On August 7, 1989, a fire started in the dump causing extensive damage (twelve million dollars) to the highway structure. Nice work, Judge. After the fire, we went for arrest warrants for Harvan and Bassi. Again, the court delayed us. I was concerned that they were going to take off, so I placed them under surveillance by my best investigators. Harvan and Bassi got wind of what we were planning, so I reached out for Dennis Massucci, my best detective, and instructed him to arrest Bassi and Harvan if they left their office trailer and went in the direction of the airport. Dennis said, "I don't think they'll go far, since all of their tires are flat." Dennis— I mean, God—works in mysterious ways. Harvan and Bassi did leave, and when they saw their flattened tires, they started to hoof it. We had more time and arrested them. The investigation was flawless and we developed an excellent RICO prosecution.

Chapter Twenty-three

Retirement from State Police

CREATION OF O.C. TASK FORCE AT CJ

In the early eighties, I was a rising star in the state police. I was a lieutenant and in an acting Captain's position and in charge of the operations of the elite Intelligence Bureau. There was no doubt that I was going to be promoted soon, and since I was in my early forties, I could have risen to Major or even higher. But, there was a problem. I didn't like the changes that were happening to the state police and I didn't like their "head in the sand" attitude. When I first went on the job, there were only two blacks and no females in the organization. The officers would tell guinea or wop jokes, and there were definitely prejudices. When I first became a trooper, I was advised that I should become a mason if I wanted to get ahead. But I was able to handle the prejudices by showing my distaste for ethnic slurs and ignoring the things that happened that didn't personally affect me. I am a very gregarious and friendly person, but I seldom socialized with troopers off duty. When I was a young detective, I submitted a report suggesting the hiring of minority troopers, especially the great need for female troopers. I didn't even receive a response. In the Newark riots, I stepped between white troopers and black citizens on numerous occasions. But the thing I liked and respected the state police for was their loyalty and their camaraderie. We were all brothers and were always there when needed by a brother. If a trooper became disabled, we would mow his lawn, take his wife shopping, and take care of all household chores. We would have someone pick him up and bring him to a barracks just to feel wanted and useful. That changed drastically in the eighties. There were different factions and jealousies developing throughout the division. The uniformed troopers resented the plainclothes troopers, and there was competition between the different sections for promotions. The Intelligence

Bureau became separate and distinct from the operational units, and the attorneys assigned to the state police pulled away and started their own division, The Division of Criminal Justice. None of these entities cooperated with each other. The state police had a mandatory retirement age of fifty-five. There was a faction of high-ranking officers who wanted the age to change to sixty-five. I started a petition against the change and ultimately won. But of course, this was revenge time. After a staff meeting, I was told to monitor and document the activities of several troopers who had disabilities because, "We have to start getting rid of these guys." That was one of the last straws for me. I was working closely with the New Jersey Commission of Investigation and my oldest son and daughter were college bound. I didn't have the money for their college and I wasn't satisfied in the direction the state police was going. The state police operational units were locked into arresting bookmakers and seldom getting to the made guys. The Intelligence Bureau would submit strategic assessments, and our operational units would ignore them. The new Division of Criminal Justice wanted to start a task force involving their attorneys and detectives from the state police to develop RICO cases, but that was rejected by the state police. I was offered an appointment as a special agent in the Commission of Investigation and I accepted, taking an early retirement from the state police. It was a heartbreaking decision, but I felt it was a sound one given the changing circumstances. After all, my goal was to destroy the Cosa Nostra (the American Mafia) and RICO was the answer. It wasn't being done by the state police. *I was with the SCI for less than a year when I received a phone call from Dort Belsole, the director of the New Jersey Division of Criminal Justice, with a job offer. He told me that he was not satisfied with the current program in the fight against organized crime and that he wanted to create a task force between the state police and the Division of Criminal Justice for the purpose of developing RICO prosecutions. He offered me a deputy chief position and my choice of staff. He was playing my song, and I immediately accepted.*

The New Jersey Division of Criminal Justice, known as CJ, was considered by the state police as its enemy. The state police believed that CJ was trying to take control of all criminal investigations in the state, thereby turning the state police into a highway patrol. This was not true, and before I took the job, I received assurance that that was not the case. I organized a task force that included the state police in every phase, but the state police refused to cooperate at first. I decided it best to just put blinders on and do the job. I first placed fifteen state investigators under my command and started recruiting experienced detectives from various law enforcement agencies. I reviewed all pending CJ cases and selected an inactive theft of fuel oil case as our first investigation. I wanted to have a test case so I could evaluate my personnel and identify their training needs. There was probable cause to obtain a court order to conduct a wiretap and there was a need for extensive surveillance, so this was the perfect case. I had two investigators who had wiretap experience, Jack Elko and Mike McGaughran, so I depended greatly on them to train the other investigators. I had no clue as to what to expect from the surveillance teams that I depended on. But I soon found out. Tankers would load up with stolen fuel oil in the early morning hours between three and five o'clock and proceed down Route 1, which is a major north/south highway. We had to identify the receivers of this stolen fuel, so that was the surveillance team's primary responsibility. Every day I would review their accomplishments only to learn that the surveillance teams were reporting that they lost sight of the tankers. How you could lose a tanker on a major highway in the early morning hours was beyond me. I called for a meeting to find out the problem. I opened the meeting by suggesting that the surveillance teams buy helium balloons with one hundred feet of cord and tie them on the bumpers of the trucks so they wouldn't lose them. I was being facetious of course, but when I heard their explanation, I almost had a fit.

Their excuse was that they were catching red lights. Unbelievable. They had no clue on how to conduct mobile surveillances and seemed quite concerned when I told them that since they were police officers involved in criminal investigations, they were allowed to slip through a red light. I then knew that I had to bring in experienced people if this task force was going to be successful. I brought in Frank Bradley, an ex-Newark police officer, and put him in charge of the surveillance teams. With the help of Frank, the investigation was a success. Soon after, the director of CJ, Don Belsole, was promoted to first assistant attorney general, and he brought back Bob Winter as director. Bob Winter was a successful prosecutor that I had worked with before. Bob Winter re-hired Bob Carroll as the chief of the Organized Crime

Task Force. Bob Carroll is an excellent attorney and one of the hardest working prosecutors I have ever met. He was and still is a good friend. I knew Carroll when he was an investigator in the Essex County prosecutor's office while attending night school to become an attorney. We had worked on many cases together, and I knew right away that we had a solid team. I recruited and hired Ron Donahue, one of the best detectives I've ever had the privilege to work with. To round out our team, we added Paul Smith, another excellent detective from Essex County, Mike McGaugran, a seasoned detective from the Monmouth County Prosecutor's Office, Ron Jivin from the NYPD, Russ Vanderbush from the Morris County Prosecutor's Office, Brian McCarthy from the Essex County Prosecutor's Office, Tom Vincent from the Public Defender's Office, and Jack Liddy and Jim Sweeney from the New Jersey state police. Later on, Steve LaPenta and James Stinsman from the Philadelphia Police Department joined the team along with old friends of mine, and good detectives from CJ, Bill Feczer and Bob Jordan, were also assigned to my command. I brought aboard a highly skilled electronic surveillance expert with a CIA experience named Eddy Tomas. We were ready to rock and roll.

In the eighties and nineties, I was in command of the investigative staff of the Statewide Organized Crime Task Force. There were twenty-eight Cosa Nostra families nationwide and seven operating in the State of New Jersey. My mission was to eliminate the families operating in New Jersey and to share intelligence with other law enforcement agencies nationally to assist in disseminating the Cosa Nostra nationally.

The task force was very successful. Our course of attack was focused on the Cosa Nostra's bread and butter, the unions, and the industries of garbage and vending as well as illicit gambling. The state police and the task force locked up bookmakers weekly, cutting off their income considerably. The profits from their bookmaking enterprises supported their army of soldiers and associates. By taking their income away, many turned to narcotics, which was against their oath. When a made man was arrested for narcotic trafficking, he would choose cooperating rather than face the death penalty imposed by his own family. This created distrust and suspicions within the Cosa Nostra. Many of the soldiers who flipped became key witnesses against their Bosses, who were prosecuted for racketeering. Turncoats such as Tommy Ricciardi, Phil Leonetti, John Januska, George Fresilone, Ira Peznick, and others gave testimony that led to the convictions of John Riggi, the Boss of the Decavalcante family, Nicky Scarfo, the Boss of the Bruno crime family, Anthony Accetturo, the Boss of the New Jersey faction of the Lucchese crime family, Bobby Bisaccia, the Capo in charge of the New Jersey faction of the Gambino crime family, and Bobby Manna, one of the Bosses of the Genovese crime family.

Chapter Twenty-four

The Cosa Nostra

THE ONLY ARMY THAT KILLS ITS OWN SOLDIERS

In nineteen seventy, Maureen Campisi, the wife of one of the notorious Campisi family members, was missing and obviously murdered. Maureen was having an affair with a made guy in the Bruno crime family, Dominick Luciano. The Campisis sought revenge against Luciano. Since Luciano was a made guy, they had to get permission from Angelo Bruno. Carmen Battaglia, the Consigliore of the Bonanno crime family and close friend of the Campisi's, brought their request to the Commission and Angelo Bruno. Since Luciano violated his oath in the Cosa Nostra by having an affair with another made man's wife, their request was approved, and on February 12, 1972, Dominick Luciano was ambushed in Roseland and shotgunned down.

The mob's killing of their own was an indicator that the Cosa Nostra was weakened and losing its discipline.

There were many gangland murders in the seventies and eighties. There were ninety-nine gangland murders in the seventies that went unsolved.

On July 16, 1972, Thomas Vito Eboli, who was the acting Boss of the Genovese crime family, was shot down. He was the highest-ranking mob figure murdered in the seventies. The reason was never known.

The Genovese crime family had a casino in Antigua that was being run by Angelo Chieppa, a large man about three hundred and fifty pounds. In 1973, he came to New Jersey by orders of the Boot, Ruggerio Bioardo, a

121

Genovese Capo regime. We found him stuffed in the trunk of a car. He was stabbed and shot to death. That was the price for skimming.

In 1974, one of the biggest numbers operators in North Jersey was Joseph Romeo, a Bruno family member. Romeo was supposed to always have large sums of cash hidden in the walls of his house. When he was gunned down, by the time the state police were called and we arrived at the house, the walls were damaged and the house was torn apart, but not one cent was found. I wonder who go the money if it was found. Another unsolved murder.

One of those who were incarcerated after pleading the fifth to the New Jersey Commission of Investigation in the late seventies was John "Johnny Coke" Lardiere, a Genovese soldier. Johnny Coke was incarcerated with Ralph "Blacky" Napoli, a Bruno Capo. They hated each other. While incarcerated, they had an argument and Johnny Coke slapped Blacky across the face. This was a major no-no. Cosa Nostra rules forbade made guys from assaulting each other. Punishment was death. On April 10, 1977, Johnny Coke received a weekend pass and stopped at a local motel where he registered for a room. As he was approaching his room, two masked men confronted him. One of the men fired a shot, but Johnny Coke didn't go down. He said, "What are you going to do now, tough guy?" He was shot again and killed. The two men saw a police car, so they dropped their hats, weapons, and holsters, and took off. Years later, I was reviewing the unsolved homicide to see which cases we could reopen now that we had DNA testing. One of my supervisors, Paul Smith, had developed information that the murder contract was carried out by Michael Coppola, who was given the opportunity to get his button for carrying out the murder contract. Michael Coppola became a significant member and the right hand for Tino Fiumaro, a Capo regime in the Genovese crime family who controlled the New Jersey port area. Paul Smith went to the Somerset County prosecutor's office and retrieved the evidence that was left at the scene. The examination of the evidence found hair fibers and a good DNA sample. We obtained a court order for Coppola to produce a sample of his DNA, but he took off. He was a fugitive for several years, and ironically, when he was finally caught and a DNA sample was collected from him, it was found to be inconclusive. He was tried and acquitted of the murder but found guilty of racketeering. I just don't get it.

Pat Marrone was suspected of using his plane to transport marijuana, but we could never prove it. He confided in Captain Sal Apuzzio about wanting to break away from Tumac and company. Sal introduced him to me and we met on a couple of occasions. He would not admit to any wrongdoings, but appeared sincere about breaking all ties with the mob. The last time we met him, he told us that he told the Taccettas that he didn't want anything to do with them. Two weeks later he was found shot to death in a car in East Orange. Years later, through the cooperation of Tumac and Tommy Ricca-iardi, we solved the murder. He was told by the Taccettas to meet them in East Orange. He brought with him a briefcase with thirty thousand dollars in it, because he thought that was what they wanted. Instead, he walked into an ambush and was shot to death. The money was still in the briefcase when his body was found. The Taccettas never looked inside.

Gangland murders continued in the nineties, as law enforcement utilizing RICO put a serious dent in the Cosa Nostra. Internal wars in the Philadel-phia crime family left over forty made guys murdered and a change in their leadership numerous times. The Colombo family had become split down the middle and started killing their own soldiers, and the Bonanno family had been expelled from the commission because of that family's involvement in narcotics. Another slap in the face of the Sicilian Mafia since the Bonnanno family's narcotic activity was with the Sicilians. The Genovese crime family continued to grow because of that family maintaining the discipline of the Mafia and its focus on the labor unions and construction.

Chapter Twenty-five

Gas Prices Go Up

THE MOB STEALS GASOLINE

The mob started stealing gasoline in a big way during the gasoline crisis in the late seventies. One of their scams was to duplicate the credit cards of major corporations. They would send a tanker to the refinery and buy the whole tank truck of gasoline and charge it to the corporation. Believe it or not, the corporations didn't even know they were getting ripped off. One evening, I received a call from a local police department. They had just arrested a guy, Joe Tobie, for bad checks, and he had told the officer that he was willing to cooperate and had information about the mob. I interviewed him and he told me that he was a driver who drove the tank trucks for the mob. It was good information, but I needed corroboration. He told me that his brother, Carmine Rivera, was also a driver, but he was in Huntsville Prison in Texas. I placed Tobie in protective custody and contacted a good friend of mine, R.D., who was an excellent detective with the Essex County Prosecutor's Office. I won't give his name, to protect his privacy. We had to hold Tobie overnight by orders of the court, so R.D. and I decided to put him and his family up for a night in a motel in Sussex County, way out in the sticks. R.D. and I took an adjoining room. We had twin beds and R.D. took the inside bed, which was the furthest from the outside. In the middle of the night I felt something whiz by my head. I awoke and there was R.D., standing alongside my bed with his face distorted. He was obviously sleep-walking but he had his thirty-eight special cocked facing toward the front

125

door, right over my head. The only thing I could think of was the next day's headline in the Star-Ledger reading "State Police Detective Bob Buccino Killed in Motel in Sussex County." I froze in my bed and started in a soft tone, saying, "R.D., R.D., R.D." until he came out of his sleep.

When he realized what was happening, he said, "Didn't you hear it? Somebody was trying to get in." Needless to say, the rest of the night I was wide-eyed listening to R.D. sawing wood. R.D. was all cop, a real cop. He was from the old school, and I had and still have a great respect and admiration for him. We did a lot of good work together, but there were also a couple of funny incidents. That's why I don't want to use his name. For instance, a couple of days later, we flew to Texas and interviewed Tobie's brother, Carmine. Carmine wasn't actually his brother. His mom and dad took Tobie in when he was a young boy and homeless and they raised him as if he was their own son. Tobie called Carmine's mother Mom and they were close, very close. Carmine told us that Huntsville was not the best place for and Italian from New Jersey to do time. He said that the blacks were treated like dogs. Next were the northerners (especially Italians), then Mexicans. Carmine decided to pretend to be Mexican, for better treatment. He was willing to cooperate if we could transfer his remaining time to New Jersey, which we did. Essex County was able to indict eight members of the Gambino and Genovese Crime families as the result of their cooperation. The trial was about to begin and the defense attorneys asked the court for the opportunity to interview Tobie, and the court agreed. I told Tobie that he had the right to refuse, but Tobie said he wasn't concerned and could handle their questions. I decided to go into the conference room with Tobie, but the defense attorneys complained. The court agreed with them and I was ordered out of the room. A couple of hours went by and I knew right then that there was a problem. When the defense attorneys came out of the room they walked over to me and said, "Your witness is a real mother fucker." I didn't know if that was good or bad. Well, it wasn't bad; it was worse than bad. The defense team got out of Tobie the fact that he had sexual intercourse with his "mom." As it turns out, he really was a mother-fucker. When his brother Carmine heard this, he was outraged and wanted to kill Tobie. He became a reluctant witness. The trial ended in a hung jury and a mistrial and the state decided not to retry it for obvious reasons. Since then, whenever I see one of the members of that defense team, I am asked if I had anymore mother-fucking witnesses. I might as well tell another funny story about R.D.

We had a loan shark victim wired up to meet his loan shark in a bar in Kearny. We had a tough time finding a parking space in close proximity to the bar so we could monitor the conversation and observe the bar. We finally found one and squeezed in. We were there a couple of minutes when R.D. announced that he had to take a shit. He refused to go into a store and told me to drive up the road a short distance where there was a park that he had taken a shit in when he was a young boy. I reluctantly gave up our parking space and drove up to the park. R.D. jumped out of the car and ran behind the bushes and took a dump. When he returned to the car I asked him how he wiped his ass. He grumpily replied, "I used my underwear." We returned to the area near the bar and finally found another parking space. After a couple of minutes, R.D. announced that he had to take another shit. Off we went again back to the park. R.D. jumped out of the car and once again went behind the bush and took a dump. The bush was only about six feet from the sidewalk. When he came back to the car I again asked him how he wiped his ass. I was especially curious this time because I knew he had used his underwear the first time. He refused to answer and I refused to let him back into the car until he told me. He finally shouted, "LEAVES!" Oh my God. Once again, back to the park. This time the only space we could find was closer to the park. We just started to monitor the conversation when I noticed two young lovers walking on the sidewalk toward the park where they stopped in front of the bush and started kissing. They soon stopped and started examining the bottom of their shoes to see if they had stepped in dog shit. Don't get mad at me, R.D.

ANGELO 'GYP' DE CARLO

Angelo was a Capo in the Genovese crime family and was part of the Boiardo crew. In 1935, Dutch Schultz, a prominent mobster, was moving in on Genovese's operations, especially the numbers racket. It was alleged that DeCarlo was part of a hit team that assassinated Schultz in a restaurant in Newark New Jersey. In 1969 the FBI released tapes from illegally bugging DeCarlo's barn (headquarters) in Mountainside, New Jersey. The recordings proved how important DeCarlo was in the Cosa Nostra. They captured conversations about several homicides he committed and about his influence in Newark politics. I met DeCarlo several times in Orange at the Berkley lounge where he liked to hang out. He looked harmless and appeared like your favorite uncle. Frankie Valli and the Four Seasons were a popular group in

Essex County. I knew them when they were the Four Lovers. Tommy DeVito, a member of the group, was into the loansharks and wasn't making his payments. DeCarlo saved DeVito from getting a beating or possibly worse. Arrangements were made for the Four Seasons to repay the loan. Jimmy Roselli, a popular singer from Hoboken, refused an appearance without getting paid. DeCarlo and the mob blackballed him and he couldn't get any work, and the DJs would not play his records. When we executed a search warrant at his house, one of my detectives used his bathroom and found a photo of Roselli in the toilet. DeCarlo would piss on him when urinating. He was a real character. When he was arrested, one of the detectives referred to him as a racketeer, and DeCarlo objected. He said he was a gangster not a racketeer. He loved that life.

ANGELO GYP DeCARLO

GAMBINO

GENOVESE

> "Although he was officially retired for a long time, he was the glue that kept it together."
>
> – A description of Simone "Sam the Plumber" DeCavalcante

LUCCHESE

RIGGI

Last of the Jersey godfathers

Dapper and courtly, Sam the Plumber was proof of Mob's power

By Robert Rudolph
STAR-LEDGER STAFF

Today, in a quiet ceremony in Mercer County, the last "godfather" will be laid to rest.

As the mourners gather in the chill of a winter morning to pay their final respects to Simone Rizzo DeCavalcante, the silver-haired mob patriarch known as Sam the Plumber, it will mark the end of an era in organized crime in New Jersey.

The others have gone: Vito Genovese, Carlo Gambino, Tommy Lucchese, the notorious bosses who founded the criminal dynasties that have controlled the American Mafia since the days of Prohibition.

DeCavalcante, 84, died Friday in a Florida hospital, the victim of a chronic heart problem. His death follows by several years the imprisonment of his hand-picked successor, John Riggi, and leaves his organization in danger of disarray.

"There are a lot of hands in the pot," one source said. "Although he was officially retired for a long time, he was the glue that kept it (the family) together." DeCavalcante had been living in Florida since 1976, after serving a brief jail term for gambling.

This week, a steady stream of family and friends — as well as members of organized crime families from New Jersey and New York — turned out to wakes at funeral homes in Elizabeth and the Princeton area to bid farewell to DeCavalcante.

No mob leader ever filled the personification of the Mafia don the way Sam the Plumber did.

The son of a Sicilian-born bootlegger, DeCavalcante rose from owner of a Trenton-area ice cream company to dapper crime lord whose photos graced newspaper fashion pages. He became the head of New Jersey's only self-contained mob family, all the while concealing his illicit activities

PLEASE SEE PATRIARCH, PAGE 9

STAR-LEDGER FILE PHOTO
Simone DeCavalcante on his way to the Federal House of Detention in New York City in 1970. He had been out of jail since 1976 and lived in Florida until his death Friday.

LAST OF THE JERSEY GODFATHERS

Chapter Twenty-six

Bobby Manna

"PLAN TO KILL" JOHN GOTTI

Bobby Manna was a rising star in the Genovese family. He was the consigliere and in the front of the line to be the next Boss. He was held in contempt for refusing to answer questions by the New Jersey Commission of Investigation in 1970. He served all his time and proved he was a stand-up guy with the LCN. When he got out, he first lived in New York and then back in Hudson County. I ordered my staff to target him, and they began surveillances of him. We identified his girlfriend's apartment where he would frequently visit in Hoboken. We focused our attention on the apartment in an attempt to develop probable cause to obtain a wiretap order. My detectives continued to bump into FBI agents. This investigation brought the FBI and my task force together, which became a very successful investigative force. This successful investigation ended Bobby Manna's career in the Genovese family.

After we completed the North Bergen investigation, we were on a roll. We received no cooperation from the state police and little from the FBI. I instructed my people that we would put our blinders on and just do our job and not worry about the politics. I assured them that if we continued making excellent cases, those agencies would come around. Eventually, they did. Cary Edwards became the attorney general and the best AG I ever had the pleasure to serve under. He recognized and appreciated the good work we were doing and did his best to get the state police to join in our effort, but he received continuous resistance.

Throughout the years, the Genovese crime family has been the most influential Cosa Nostra family in New Jersey. Not only did they have the most made guys of all of the families in New Jersey, but they also had a strong influence in the garbage, vending, and construction industries.

Their control of the New Jersey waterfront has been the most lucrative for that family in all the years. Louis "Bobby" Manna, the consigliere and a graduate of the SCI's contempt school, came back into New Jersey to develop the New Jersey Hudson River coastline, which was being referred to as the Gold Coast of New Jersey. There were numerous lucrative construction contracts planned, and there was the creation of an upscale development called "Newport City". Bobby Manna and his crew planned to get as much as they could from these projects. After all, they controlled the concrete and construction unions in Hudson County. As soon as I heard that Bobby was back in town and was staying on most nights at a close female friend's apartment, I put my investigators on him around the clock. We were just at the point where we were getting enough probable cause to initiate electronic monitoring when my people advised me that they were constantly running into FBI agents who appeared to also be surveilling Manna. I called for a sit down with the FBI and I set up the criteria for both agencies on how to proceed in a joint effort. It was simple; the agency that was the furthest along in their investigation would become the lead agency, and the other would provide manpower and resources to assist the lead agency. Well, it turned out that the FBI had already prepared a title three, which is their wiretap order, so I committed our resources to assist. Of course the FBI said we were fifty/fifty partners. What they meant by fifty/fifty was that I would put up most of the manpower and resources and the FBI would give the press release. Anyway, it was a very successful investigation, even though the FBI took most of the credit. Conversations that were intercepted indicated that Bobby Manna and the Genovese family were plotting to kill the infamous Gambino crime family Boss John Gotti in retaliation for the murder of his previous Boss, Big Paulie Castellano. In one of the conversations we intercepted, Bobby Manna made reference to their ten-year plan to reap the profits from the construction in the Gold Coast. The Cosa Nostra had a ten year plan and law enforcement has a hard time planning a year at a time. The convictions of Bobby Manna, Jimmy Napoli, Marty Casella, John Derrico, Richard DeSciscio, and Rocco Napoli, and at the same time the conviction of the heads of the Cosa Nostra families in New York by the New York Authorities certainly put an end to their ten-year plan. As a result of this investigation, we received the respect of the FBI and subsequently a memorandum of understanding between the New Jersey Organized Crime and Racketeering Bureau and the FBI was created. I served on the policy board and we began monthly meetings to avoid duplication and to combine our efforts toward a common goal to eliminate the Cosa Nostra. This lasted until the change of our administration. When Governor Florio was elected Governor, the FBI discontinued our meetings. The only reason I could think of was that Governor Florio was an Italian American, and the FBI's mindset about Italians was too much for them to handle. I remember Agent Bob Lenihan and Agent Dennis Marcholonis asking me one question shortly after the governor's election, "Bob, do you have to report to the governor?" I told them that I reported to the new attorney general Bob DelTufo, who was an ex-United States attorney and a man of the highest integrity, and he reported to the governor. So indirectly, I reported to the governor. Our meetings were discontinued shortly thereafter. Shame on them.

ANTHONY "LITTLE PUSSY" RUSSO

Chapter Twenty-seven

The Decavalcante Family

When Luck Luciano created the five New York families, he also created the New Jersey and Philadelphia families. At first, he was going to create a family based in Newark, but decided on creating one out of New Brunswick since it was more centralized in the state. To start the family, Filipo Amari was recruited from Ribera Sicily. He brought with him a group of Sicilian Mafioso, and a small family was born. In the mid-sixties, one of Amari's trusted soldiers, Sam DeCavalcante, became the Boss. DeCavalcante increased the membership of the family by recruiting more soldiers from Ribera Sicily. DeCavalcante ruled the family until 1976 where, after doing time, in 1982 he retired to Florida and turned the reins over to John Riggi. The family's power came from their control over the International Association of Laborers and Hod Carriers in New Jersey. In 1990, John D'Amato became the Boss. He was murdered in 1992 and Jake Amari became the Boss. After he died in 1997 the family was run by a ruling panel. In 2000, the FBI came up with a major indictment against the hierarchy, and the code of omerta no longer existed in this family. The family is almost non-existent with the membership down to less than one fifth of what it was in the early days of about fifty soldiers.

I had an investigation on John Riggi in the late seventies when he was the acting Boss. I received a complaint from the corporate owners of a new Sheraton Hotel that opened on Route 1 directly across from the Newark Airport. It was a non-union hotel and the management was receiving a lot of pressure to unionize. There was a suspicious fire in one of the elevators and they found a snake in their pool. The management would not bend, and a meeting was being arranged to meet with John Riggi. Riggi had requested that the meeting be held at lunchtime in the hotel's restaurant. I got a court order and bugged the table they were going to meet at. Attending the meeting were Riggi, the hotel manager, and the corporate attorney (good old boy from Roanoke, Virginia) who told me prior to the meeting that there was no way they were going to unionize. This was a brand new hotel, and they had just opened their restaurant, which was unusually packed for lunch that particular day. Every table was full of men. When they met and after they introduced themselves, the only thing John Riggi said was, "Gentlemen, New Jersey is a pro union state." With that, every table of men, one at a time, stood up and walked over to John Riggi and said, "Mr. Riggi, good afternoon." One by one, they introduced themselves by name and said what local union they were from, and then they left the restaurant. After their lunch and nothing but small talk, I met in a room with the two Sheraton representatives, and the Good Old Boy asked me one question: "Is this John Riggi really in the Mafia?" I answered that he was, but for them not to worry about that, I assured them that we in law enforcement wanted to arrest him. Our meeting ended with the corporate attorney telling me he was going back to Roanoke and would meet with the board of directors and would call me the following Monday. I did not receive the phone call so I waited a couple of days and called Roanoke, only to be told that the board of directors decided to let the union in. I guess Riggi successfully showed his power.

It has been implied that the HBO show "The Sopranos" was based on the DeCavalcante family. I must admit, there are many similarities.

The Commission Trial

In the mid-eighties, law enforcement using RICO decimated the Cosa Nostra. Throughout the United States, the hierarchy of Organized Crime was being prosecuted and given lengthy sentences. Faced with dying in jail, many broke the code of omerta, causing a breakdown of the once proud discipline that held the Cosa Nostra together.

One of the most significant prosecutions ever developed was the prosecution of the leadership of the five New York families in nineteen eighty six. A young United States attorney who prosecuted this famous case was Rudolph Giuliani, who was quoted as saying, "Our approach is to wipe out the five families." Although Giuliani, who is Italian American, and the FBI received most of the credit, there were two detectives within the NYPD who actually developed the case. The original defendants were Gambino Boss Paul "Big Paul" Castellano who was murdered by John Gotti in December 1986, Anthony "Fat Tony" Salerno, Boss of the Genovese family, Carmine "Junior" Persica, Boss of the Colombo family, Anthony "Duck" Corallo, Boss of the Lucchese family, and Philip "Rusty" Rastelli, Boss of the Bonanno family.

Many of their Underbosses and consigliore were also convicted leaving a serious void in the leadership of the five Cosa Nostra families that not only had strong influence in New York, but also in New Jersey, Connecticut, Pennsylvania, and the surrounding states.

Chapter Twenty-eight

John Digilio

John DiGilio from Bayonne, a prominent soldier in the Genovese crime family, was a street-tough ex-pug who ruled Hudson County with an iron fist. He was known for his volatile temper and was quite an earner for the family for many years. In 1975 he and about eight defendants were on trial in federal court for loan sharking and other offenses. By the time the trial got started, several of his co-defendants were found murdered, gangland style.

DiGilio tried to feign that he was nuts, but it didn't work, and the trial was ready to begin when the federal judge received a letter allegedly written by a disgruntled FBI agent. In the letter, the writer alleged that the FBI and the United States Attorney's Office had illegally bugged the offices of the defense attorneys in an attempt to find out about their defense strategies. The letter named two attorneys whose offices were bugged, one in Long Branch and the other in Orange. The federal judge decided that he couldn't call upon the FBI or the U.S. attorney's office since the allegations were against them, so he called upon the state police. Detective Charlie Coe and I were assigned to investigate. The first thing we did was contact the attorneys who were named and request an examination of their offices by our experts. The attorney from Orange, who was a good friend of mine and a prominent attorney, refused, telling me that he didn't care if his office was bugged, and in fact always believed it was anyway. When we contacted the Long Branch attorney, he told us that he had already found the bug. He said he had called George Weingarten, an ex-Bayonne Police Officer who worked for John

DiGilio and, in later years, was implicated in the gangland murder of DiGilio. Weingarten recommended that he call Sirchie, an electronic expert from Conshohocken, Pennsylvania. When the attorney contacted the expert, he received instruction over the phone and was able to find the bug that was a duplex electrical outlet with a transmitter in it. This was the beginning of one of the most bizarre investigations I ever had. The cast of Damon Runyon characters consisted of a hunchback, a Hawaiian 007, a cop who went bad, a homosexual, and a ruthless mob guy. As soon as I saw the duplex receptacle, I knew that the manufacturer was Frank Chin of New York. I had met him a couple of times and saw his work. His specialization was duplex receptacles. Charlie and I took the receptacle to Frank Chin for identification, and when we did, Frank immediately identified it as the one he sold Sirchie from Conshohocken, Pennsylvania. Yes, the same guy the attorney from Long Branch had called. I asked Frank how he knew that was the one, since he sold thousands of them. He said because it was defective and was taken out of the junk heap. He then called his assistant, who came out of the back room dragging his foot. He had a hunchbacked assistant who we immediately labeled Quasimodo. The hunchback corroborated Fran Chin's account of what happened. He said that Sirchie didn't want to spend much money because, he told him, "It was meant to be found," so he didn't even care if it worked. So they took one out of the rejected bin and sold it to him. Frank Chin was a flamboyant Asian man who bragged about his work with the DEA and CIA. He was very friendly with a noted mystery author whose name I won't mention, even though he died a few years ago. Frank had a photograph of the author's beautiful wife lying in a coffin and offered me the opportunity to have sex with her, but she only flicked in a coffin. Um—no thanks. Frank Chin became our key witness. Charlie and I then went to Conshohocken, Pennsylvania to visit Mr. Sirchie. There was a technician named Bill who worked for Sirchie. We received little cooperation. Sirchie admitted to knowing George Weingarten and admitted to buying duplex receptacles from Frank Chin. He said the call from the attorney from Long Branch was just a coincidence and that Charlie and I would still have to find someone who could place the receptacle in George Weingarten's hands. A United States Grand Jury was empaneled, so we subpoenaed Sirchie and his staff, including Bill, to Newark to appear before a federal grand jury. One attorney represented them all. They had left Bill alone at one point, so I walked over to him. He was slumped in a chair and I asked him what was wrong. He said, "I want to tell you the truth, but I can't. They said I would get a pair of cement shoes if I say anything." I asked him if he told his attorney, and he said that he couldn't, because the attorney wasn't his by choice. I immediately went into see the United States attorney, Jonathan Goldstein, a tough, no-nonsense prosecutor. I told him what had occurred and he told me to bring Bill into his office and to place him in protective custody. So I did. While walking over to the Goldstein's Office, the attorney who came with Sirchie approached us and asked where I was taking Bill. I asked Bill in front of the attorney, "Is he representing you?" and Bill answered that he wasn't. I continued into Goldstein's Office. The attorney actually started banging on the door, asking for his client. After several minutes and a brief discussion with Bill, Jonathan Goldstein invited the attorney in and told him that he was not Bill's attorney and that Bill was placed in the protective custody of the government and that the attorney would have to leave the premises without Bill.

I had a lot of experience getting the federal government to place witnesses in the Federal Witness Protection Program, but never as fast as in this case. Bill was a tough witness to protect. In fact, he was disgusting. He had prior arrests for soliciting teenaged boys to his apartment. He wore female panties and had no control of his rectal muscles. He would fart when he walked and would have occasional bowel movements accidentally. Despite all of this, Bill became a key witness for us. He implicated George Weingarten, identifying him as the one who ordered the receptacle that was meant to be found from Serchie. He told us that after Charlie Coe and I visited Sirchie in Pennsylvania, Sirchie told Weingarten. When DiGilio heard about it, he ordered Weingarten and his attorney "My Cousin Vinny," to go to Pennsylvania and get a statement from Sirchie, which they did. When they came back to Bayonne, DiGilio wasn't satisfied and ordered them back to Pennsylvania to record the statement. When the attorney told DiGilio that they hadn't even had dinner yet, DiGilio threw them both a banana and told them that that was their dinner and they'd better get the statement right. The FBI then busted a female clerk who admitted to stealing the FBI stationary that was used to write the fraudulent letter to the judge. We had made a pretty good case. We had some physical evidence, circumstantial evidence, and two fact witnesses.

Just before the trial began, Frank Chin, who refused protection, closed shop one night and walked to the garage to get his Mercedes. The car had a flat, so he went back into the building to call for help. When the elevator opened, he was hit with several bullets to the head, killing him instantly. The cigarette was still in his mouth. Bill was relocated to a New England state where he was arrested for soliciting the chief of police's teenaged son for sex. Most of the charges had to be dropped, but DiGilio was convicted in federal court with several of his subordinates. His sentence was later reduced and he was out in less than a year. Years later, DiGilio was murdered gangland style and dumped in the river by the Meadowlands. Weingarten was indicted for the murder but committed suicide before the trial began. Chin's murder was never solved. We knew who did it but didn't have the evidence to convict anyone. Another day in the naked city.

The Commission of Investigation (SCI) had an excellent staff, and I became part of their team immediately. Although small, they did some great work. I became a little disenchanted because I was told that the reason they were hiring me was they wanted to resume their attack against organized crime that made that agency respected in the late sixties and early seventies. The first thing I did upon my arrival was to submit a report outlining the threat of the Cuban and Colombian Narcotic Operations and suggested that the SCI subpoena the leaders of these operations just as they did with the Cosa Nostra (Italian) mob leaders, but this proposal was rejected. It was letdown for me. However, I was assigned to the boxing probe. The SCI was trying to identify organized crime's influence in professional boxing. I had to serve a subpoena on John DiGilio, a Genovese soldier from Bayonne and an ex-pug himself. It was the week of Christmas, so I called his attorney, Larry Bronson, and asked him if he could have DiGilio at his office so I could serve him. At first, Bronson played coy with me, but when I told him that I didn't want to serve DiGilio at his mother's home on Christmas Eve, he was receptive and we arranged service to be Christmas Eve at Bronson's law office in Bayonne. I wasn't sure where his office was located, so I arrived in Bayonne early and found his office almost an hour before our scheduled meeting. I was dressed in a sport jacket with a black pullover shirt. When I arrived, the office, which was an old store with a large glass window front, wasn't opened, but I could see a black associate lawyer of Bronson's on the phone. I tapped the window and he motioned to me that he would be with me in a couple of minutes. It was cold outside, so I tapped again. Finally, with phone in hand, he walked over and let me in. While on the phone, another phone rang and, putting the one caller on hold, he answered the second phone. It was John DiGilio calling. The attorney became extremely nervous and cut off the first caller. I was standing right in front of his desk as he stood behind the desk talking to "the Boss." Not knowing who I was, he said to DiGilio, "Don't worry, John. This 'Bookino' is an asshole. He's nothing but a delivery boy. Get this subpoena quashed. I'll handle this asshole." While he was talking, I was motioning him to talk to me. Finally, he put his hand over the mouthpiece of the phone and asked, "What?"

"I'm the asshole you're waiting for." He fell back into his chair and, stuttering, said to DiGilio, "I think he's here now; I'll call you back." He looked at me and had a hard time speaking.

I said, "Don't worry, I won't tell DiGilio that you were talking to him and letting me hear your conversation."

With that, Larry Bronson came into the office. He took one look at his associate and said, "What happened to you? You're as white as me. Did you see a ghost or something?"

The black attorney answered, "I though Mr. Buccino was one of DiGilio's guys."

Bronson responded, "Buccino is too well dressed to be one of John's guys. He looks more like one of Tino's guys." He was referring to Tino Fiumara, a Capo in the Genovese family. I saw the black attorney from time and he really was always very cordial to me. I wonder why?

TUMAC

Anthony "Tumac" Accetturo rose through the ranks of the Cosa Nostra as I rose through the ranks in the state police. He ran his New Jersey operations from Florida and occasionally would meet his crew in New York when he went to see his Bosses in the Lucchese crime family. Tumac had been arrested several times in Florida but always beat the raps by playing nuts. He would share his technique with John DiGilio who also was playing nuts in New Jersey. Years later when Tumac agreed to cooperate, playing nuts created a problem for him. Because he was deemed nuts in Florida, we couldn't use his testimony in New Jersey. When told about this, Tumac told us that he did have "old-timers" disease. But while he was on trial in New Jersey, he slipped in the shower and hit his head, causing an immediate return of his memory.

Several years ago, John DiGilio was subpoenaed to appear before the state grand jury. I was scheduled to be the next witness, and while waiting in the hallway when John was testifying, I heard a commotion coming from the Grand Jury Room. The jurors were hurried from the room and an excited deputy attorney general came out and asked me to call for someone from the lab to come to the grand jury room to collect evidence. John had claimed to have pissed his pants. There was water on the floor by the witness chair and the front of his pants were wet. The lab technician arrived and took a sample of the water and it was determined to be urine. John did piss his pants. Another time, John was indicted for loan sharking and was on trial in Morris County. I was scheduled to give expert testimony against John, and he was trying every maneuver to keep me off the stand. John got sick a couple of times, thus delaying testimony. One of his men served me with a civil complaint alleging harassment. George Weingarten, John's trusted assistant who later killed DiGilio, actually approached me in the hallway and asked me if I wanted to become police director in Bayonne. What a trip this guy was. One day during a recess and after being there for over a week and still not getting on the stand, I said to the deputy attorney general, "How long do you think it will be before I take the stand? I'm running out of clean shirts."

John heard me and shouted, "The mob has been buying your shirts for years. I could buy you a couple." Of course this was a lie and he just stupidly said that to get me mad and embarrass me before I testified. It worked. I blew my top and told him to come closer and I'd show him that he was not that tough because I would knock him on his ass." He made my Italian blood boil. The DAG grabbed me and brought me into a room to cool down. John pointed a finger at me and said, "Got you!" Finally, it was my turn to testify. As soon as I took the stand, John did a passing out routine and fell off his chair onto the floor. While lying there I motioned with my hand as if I was counting him out. I'm lucky I wasn't held in contempt.

Peter R. "Petey White" Campisi, left, preceded his cousin, Peter S. "Petey Black" Campisi, in death by two years, furthering the mob family's decline.

PHOTO - THE CAMPISIS, BIAGGIO PETEY WHITE PETEY BLACK

DIGILIO

JOHN DIGILIO

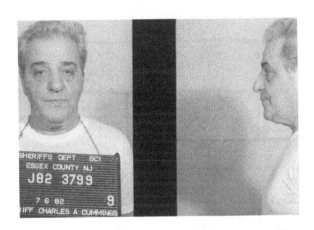

BLAGGIO CAMPISI

Chapter Twenty-nine

Campisi and Gallicchios

THE SCUM OF COSA NOSTRA

When I became a police officer, whenever a wise guy would tell me that they never did anything to hurt the Italian neighborhoods, I felt like smacking them. I would remind them about Newark, the Campisis, and the Gallicchios.

In the late eighties, I assigned Paul Smith's team and Bobby Hayes, who was one of my most aggressive investigators, to take out the Gallicchios. The Gallicchio family was a renegade group headquartered in the Vailsburg section of Newark on the East Orange line. They were blood related and were despised by most of the other families, although they were known to do some "work" for the Cosa Nostra families. Louis Gallicchio, Sr. who was born in 1940, was the leader of this family and was known to have carried out some strong arm for the Lucchese crime family. He was a close friend of Anthony Acceturo and Michael and Marty Taccetta. Louie had some unusual habits for a so-called wise guy. I would rather not include them in my book, but if you want to know what they are, just ask anybody who served time with him. His older brother, Nicholas "Monkey," had served time for the murder of a Newark police officer, but our wonderful judiciary let him out of jail so he could continue his life as a racketeer.

After a year of undercover work and wiretaps, we concluded by arresting Louis Sr., who got eighteen years in State Prison. Louie didn't mind prison because they were full of guys who liked to indulge in his unusual habit. Louie's son, Louis, Jr., got five years in state prison. His brother, Monkey, received a fifty-year state sentence because of his lengthy criminal record. Michael Galliccho received a six-year sentence in State Prison. Louie Gallicchio's wife, Catherine, received two years' probation. Nicholas Gallicchio, Jr. received three years' probation. We also arrested twenty two members of their crew for various narcotic offenses.

Among the twenty two was John Redman of Maplewood, who was a victim of an organized crime hit by the Lucchesis in July of 1990. We dug up his body in 1993 in Ocean County. Also included was Nicholas DelViscovo of Livingston, who was given a sentence of a minimum of twenty-four and a half years for his assault on State Investigator Paul Smith and an FBI Agent. The two officers were run over when DelViscovo attempted to resist his arrest by the officers.

When the arrests began, we started with Louie Gallicchio and his niece, Francine, and attempted to flip them. I had to call in one of my new female investigators, Patti, to search Francine, who was not too clean in appearance. It was sad to see because she really was a good looking girl, and I wondered what kind of chance she had due to the family she grew up in. This was Patti's first organized crime roundup, and I called her to come to work early in the morning. She arrived all dolled up. She was a very attractive lady and she was meticulously dressed. When she reported for work, I told her to take Francine into the bathroom and strip-search her. Patti had a shocked expression on her face. She took one look at Francine and started to gag. She apologetically told me that she "just couldn't do it." I apolitically reminded her of her responsibility as a law enforcement officer. Poor Patti. She survived the action and today is a very effective officer.

Louie refused to cooperate, so I gave the order to proceed with the other arrests. We had state police SWAT team "TEAMS" hit the Gallicchio's home on Smith Street because Monkey was a cop killer and they had a pit bull dog as well as a rottweiler. I explained the situation to the state police sergeant, who was about five foot eight and all muscle, about the two dangerous vicious dogs. He didn't seem one bit concerned. Bobby Hayes went in with the TEAMS Unit and reported later that when they entered the house, the sergeant went in low and had a claw type instrument in his hand. When the pit bull attacked, the sergeant clawed the mouth of the pit bull, lifted him off the floor, and slammed him, causing the dog to cower. The Rottweiler saw what happened to the pit bull and pissed and shit before hiding under the bed. Another great job by the New Jersey state police.

After entry was completed, the arrests were made. I received a call from Bobby Hayes from inside the house. Bobby informed me that Louie wanted to talk to me. Louie got on the phone and said, "Buccino, you are from the old neighborhood, please, you have to do me a favor and we'll cooperate. Tell your investigator to stop stepping on my mother's head."

I said, "Put him on the phone." Bobby Hayes got on the phone huffing, and our conversation went like this: Me: "Bobby, are you stepping on their mother's head?"

Hayes: "She was resisting."
Me: "STOP stepping on her head."
Hayes: "Oh, OK."

Through the years, the Gallicchios have introduced many to the world of drugs. They exploited the black and Hispanic communities in Newark using fear, intimidation, and even murder to achieve their goals. Their family predecessors were the first to bring hardcore drugs into Newark, East Orange, and the surrounding towns. Just take a drive through Central Newark, East Orange, Irvington, and Orange, and see for yourself what drugs have done in those areas. Incarceration of the Gallicchios is not good enough. May they rot in hell. Their grandfather, Jerry "the Boot" Gallicchio, was a member of the Sicilian Mafia and was one of the Sicilians arrested for distributing heroin in 1957. Years later, when I became chief of detectives in the Union County prosecutor's office, and the Gallichio's had completed their sentences and returned to the Vailsburg section of Newark, my Narcotics Strike Force arrested the Gallicchios again. They just won't go away.

In the mid-fifties, heroin was distributed by the Sicilian Mafia. They hit the streets in Newark and its surrounding communities. Jerry "the Boot" Gallicchio, a member of the Sicilian Mafia, was arrested and convicted as being part of that distribution network. One thing we've learned about the Cosa Nostra is that they are resilient and have the ability to change with the times. Through the years, members of the Gallicchio family have been arrested for many narcotic trafficking offenses. One was even convicted of the murder of a police officer.

The Union County Prosecutor's Office's Narcotics Strike Force, under the supervision of Assistant Prosecutor Jim Tansey and then-Detective Sergeant Mike Burns commenced an extensive investigation on the Gallicchio narcotics distribution enterprise. Detective Christopher Gulbin led a team of investigators from the Union County prosecutor's office, the DEA, state police, FBI, and the municipal police departments in this complex investigation. When Detective Christopher Gulbin, the lead investigator whose information initiated this investigation, identified the Gallicchios and the fact that this OxyContin distribution operation was controlled by the Cosa Nostra, organized crime expert DAG Bob Codey from the Division of Criminal Justice joined our task force and contributed immensely to the success of this operation. This six- month investigation identified a massive OxyContin distribution network operating in three states under the control of Louis Gallicchio and his associates, some of whom are members of the Lucchesi and Bonnanno Crime Families and the notorious Bloods street gang. Over two thousand tablets, which had a street value of two hundred thousand dollars, were distributed weekly, many to several colleges in the Boston area where students were paying as much as one hundred dollars per pill.

On November 11, 2004, over a hundred law enforcement officers in three states made twenty-four arrests and seized over 20,000 OxyContin tablets valued at over two million dollars.

I was honored to present awards to these guys for their efforts in the success of this investigation and hopefully the end of the Gallicchio criminal enterprise once and for all.

The Campisi's were a violent renegade group from South Orange Avenue in Newark. They committed every crime imaginable. They ran gambling houses, sold drugs, and committed armed robberies. You name it, and they did it. They also had a couple of vicious killers in their group: Ira Peznick, a Russian Jew who liked to kill, and John Tully, an Irishman who also enjoyed the sport. One of the murders they committed was of their "best friend," Candido Treuba. The state police, after a long investigation, made numerous arrests of the Campisi group. One trooper got Pesnick to cooperate, and Tully followed. It was my job to interview Tully to evaluate his cooperation. When he described the murder of Candido Treuba, I was convinced that he shouldn't get a deal from the state. He told me that Candy was his best friend. They grew up together and he loved the guy, but the Campisi's thought he was a rat, so he was given the contract. He and Ira told Candy they were going to a craps game in Hillside. They just drove around and found a quiet street where they said the game was. When they got out of the car, Tully pulled out his gun and shot Candy in the chest. Candy grabbed

Tully and said, "Not you. Not you." Tully told me he just shot him again until he was dead. As he told me the story, he never blinked. His eyes were cold and he showed no emotion. That was enough for me. I turned him down. He served time and believe it or not, when he got out and went out west and surfaced years later, he became mayor of a small town. Peznick was relocated and had a panic attack and died of a heart attack. At least they said it was a panic attack. His shoes were a message to his wife that he was OK.

Peter "PayPay" Campisi was a made guy in the Gambino crime family. He was the son of Anthony "NayNay" Campisi, another made guy. Peter was running a game in Staten Island, and in the early morning hours on July 18, 1983, Peter was gunned down after he left his game. Anthony got his revenge. On August 18, 1983 Albert "Tiny" Manzo's large three hundred and fifty-pound body was found in the trunk of a car in Hillside.

PHOTO - BOBBY CABERT

Chapter Thirty

Cabert

Bobby "Cabert" Biscarcia, for years an enforcer for the Gambino crime family, became the infamous John Goth's main Caporegime in New Jersey. He took over the area once controlled by Joseph Paterno and Mike Mandaglia. He could never fill their shoes. Cabert was a degenerate gambler and gambled away his money faster than he could make it. He was feared and known for his quick temper and his lack of conscience when it came to murder. He was well liked and respected by the other families especially Michael Taccetta and the Lucchese crime family. Andy Gerard, Caporegime in the Genovese crime family, had a live and let live attitude toward Cabert. Cabert was actually a very funny guy. He was quite friendly with Joe Pesci, and the role Pesci played in Goodfellas was rumored to be that portraying Bobby Cabert. There was one scene when Pesci was in a nightclub and Ray Liotta told him that he made him laugh and Pesci responded, pretending that he was mad by saying something like, "I make you laugh? What am I, a clown to you?" Ray Liotta became nervous and tried to explain his remarks when Pesci laughed, held a gun to his head, and said it was a joke. The rumor was that Cabert did the same thing to Pesci in a restaurant. While we were investigating Cabert, he called Joe Pesci to have lunch with him at the Belmont Tavern where chicken savoy was made famous. Guess where Pesci went? To the Belmont.

The Gambino family had lost a lot of their influence in New Jersey, and Cabert certainly was not known for his leadership qualities. During our eleventh-month investigation we utilized ten wiretaps and several room bugs. This investigation was successful and it certainly had its humorous, memorable moments. Cabert lived in a condo in Nutley and he had special pick-proof locks on his doors. We had obtained a court order to install several bugs, but had difficulty in picking the locks. Our expert tried several times but was unsuccessful. We even brought in an expert from New York and he was unable to make entry. To install a bug is not an easy task. First, I had to place the target under surveillance to be sure that he wouldn't return home while we were making our installation. We had to make certain that our entry was clean and undetectable. We would also have to make certain that our bugs were strategically placed so we could have good audibility. We had failure after failure to make entrance to his condo, and after at least five attempts, we thought we had a solution. Our ex-CIA tech expert believed he made a key that would work. He and Paul Smith were at the front door as I sat in a Cadillac parked across the road, monitoring the surveillance teams and backing up the entry team. Jack Liddy, a retired Captain in the New Jersey state police, accompanied me. Jack was the Will Rodgers of the state police. When I called him and asked him if he wanted to come out of retirement, he never asked me the salary or work conditions. He simply said, "Thank you very much." While we were monitoring the entry team, Jack said something to me that summed up our careers. He asked me, "What are the best movies?"

I answered, "Movies about the mob." He continued to ask me about TV shows, books, and other publications, and I answered the same way. "Mob stories are the most successful."

He said, "Could you imagine? We actually lived all those stories. It can't be better than that." I could see our entry team fumbling around the front door. It was obvious that the key was not working. Paul Smith looked over to me and motioned that it wasn't working. Then I saw Paul open a window and crawl his skinny body into the condo. There was an unlocked window. No one ever tried the windows. All that trouble and all we had to do was open a window. I guess you live and learn. Every Saturday, John Gotti expected his Capos to visit him at either the Ravenite Social Club or the Bergen Hunt and Fish Club. Cabert would bring a tray of chicken savoy from the Belmont Tavern or Joe Rackets would cook up a tray of gutana (pork skin) or stuffed bonnet. John Gotti expected a boost from his Capos on his birthday and on Christmas. Christmas called for at least five thousand dollars. Bobby Cabert was broke and Christmas was a couple of weeks away. He owed his bookmaker around forty thousand dollars, and he didn't have the five thousand dollar la boost for Gotti. We decided to arrest his bookmaker, and it was the first bookmaker I have ever arrested who didn't reopen the next day. So Cabert owed the money and couldn't bet to get even. One of the Cosa Nostra rules was that all made men, including Bossed, had to pay their gambling debts, so Cabert could not pull his weight with the bookmaker and say, "Forget about it." Cabert had planned a hijacking of a load of cigarettes, which he had already sold. This would give him enough money to pay the bookie, give Gotti his five thousand dollars, and have plenty left over for the holidays. Since we were on his wire when they hijacked the tractor trailer, we knew where they were unloading the cigarettes. We swooped in and arrested eight members of Cabert's crew and seized the cigarettes. Now Cabert was not only broke, but he had to arrange bail for his crew. A week before he was expected to go to New York with the five thousand dollars, he received a call from Arnold Squiteiri, another Capo in the Gambino family, and the conversation went like this:

Arnold — "Bobby, Merry Christmas, are you ready for New York?"

Cabert — "Merry Christmas, Merry Christmas. That mother fucking Santa Claus! I have eight pincherimises, a ricking bookie I owe big time. The motherfucker closed shop. He should get a cell phone and sit on top of Yogi Berra's health joint with a peacock." Mother fucker Santa Claus., the mother flickers are on every street corner in the world. You can't even whack them. If there were only one or two, we could whack them and it would be all over, but they are on every corner. They have Jew Santa Clauses, Puerto Rican Santa Claus; they even have a black Santa Claus. The mother fuckers are all over. That fucking Hitler. That mother fucker couldn't finish the job right. The fucking Jews run Christmas." He went on and on.

Arnold - "I feel sorry for the guy that crosses you today."

I called this recording "The Conspiracy to Kill Santa Claus." Well, Cabert was glomming money from everyone. What he didn't know was that his loyal crew was warning others when Cabert was around so they could avoid him. We ended up arresting Cabert and his entire crew for racketeering, which included extortion, hijacking, gambling, and attempted burglary.

During our investigation, we uncovered a scheme by Cabert and his trusted soldier Sam "Little Sammy" Corsaro where they planned to break into my office and set fire to our evidence. They never pulled it off. I guess they figured that since we had guns too, they might lose. You see, they only have balls when they are the only ones with the guns. During the trial, they tried everything possible to disrupt the prosecution. The majority of our jurors were black; one female was a single parent of a young boy. One Saturday while she was getting her car washed, an unknown male who appeared to be of Italian decent approached her and, while rubbing the top of her son's head, simply said, "You have a good boy here. I hope nothing bad happens to him because of his mother. You know what I mean?" Another juror's car was shot up while parked in front of her house. An assistant prosecutor's father's home was hit with a shotgun blast.

Days ago, Mr. Marra asked me the same question, and I answered, "It was a judgment. Mr. Marra tried to mock me in this courtroom."

Marra jumped up, objecting that he didn't try to mock me, and one of the jurors shouted out, "Oh, yes you did."

I continued by saying, "Mr. Marra read definitions from a two-foot deep dictionary, and none of his definitions were similar to the one I gave. I would hate to believe that Mr. Marra tried to deceive this court, but when I went home that evening, I looked in my little dictionaries (pulling them out of my pocket as I spoke) and I proceeded to read the definitions, which were all similar to the one I gave to the court." I ended by saying, "I guess I do know the definition of opinion." The jury was laughing and, during the break, Tom Ashley said, "Buccino, you're good. I don't know how I got sucked into that."

Another time, Marra criticized my credentials as an expert and the lack of books that I had read, so during lunch I wrote down all the organized crime cases I had worked on and the knowledge I gained from each case. When we went back into the courtroom and cross resumed on my qualifications, I pulled out the list, to the objections of Marra. The wishy-washy judge agreed with Marra that I shouldn't be allowed to introduce that document during the trial, and I was admonished by the court. It didn't matter much, because the court still qualified me as an expert and I gave expert testimony.

But I figured I might as well have some fun with it, so I wrote myself another note and put it in my top pocket. During cross by Marra, I gave the appearance that I was having difficulty with one of his questions and would look into the audience and then pull the note from my pocket, look at it, and then answer the question. Marra objected and made a motion to the court that since I was referring to some notes, he wanted me to provide those notes to the court. The judge ordered me to provide the court with the note. It read, "Honey, bring home a loaf of bread and a pound of bologna."

Marra was also a screamer and would approach the witness chair and slam papers in front of me. He did it once too often. He got in my face and I calmly said, "Mr. Marra, I don't mind you're shouting and slamming papers in front of me, but I suggest you change your mouthwash; your breath is killing me." Marra walked backward with a shocked look on his face and then shouted, "You big goof! How would you like a punch in the mouth?"

I answered, "Why are you walking away from me? Come over here if you want to punch me in the mouth." Little Sammy Corsaro jumped up and called me a punk. I told him to "Sit down, you little pip squeak, what do you think you're going to do?" He sat down faster than he got up. Marra was ranting and shouting as he walked toward me. I leaned back and, with one hand obstructing the judge's view, I moved my mouth as if speaking the word "Gavone," an Italian expression that means slob. Marra shouted out, "Judge, he just told me to go fuck myself." I didn't, but the judge said he saw it too, and chewed me out. There was an appeal in an attempt to call a mistrial, but the court denied the motion for a mistrial.

The only defendant who was acquitted was Joe "Rackets" Casiere. It didn't bother me, because Joe was a gambler and a dice mechanic. I never heard of his involvement in any violence, and he was a hell of a cook. One time he gave his recipe for bonzet (stuffed breast of veal); I still use that recipe. Thanks, Joe. The rest received heavy sentences, and Cabert was later tried and convicted of a murder in New York on orders of John Gotti and Sammy the Bull.

Chapter Thirty-one

The Iceman

In the early eighties, a young state police detective, Pat Kane, was investigating Richard Kuklinski, a suspect in several murder cases including Paul L. Hoffman, Gary Thomas Smith, George Malliband, Danny Deppner, Robert Prongay, Louis Masgay, and Roy DeMao, a Cosa Nostra Gambino crime family Caporegime. In 1981, Louis Masgay left his home to meet Kuklinski in Little Ferry to buy blank video tapes. He was carrying a large amount of money. He never returned home. He was found two years later in New York State. Interestingly, the medical examiner found ice in Masgay's internal organs. His body had been frozen prior to being dumped in New York. Kuklinski was immediately dubbed "The Iceman." Detective Kane had identified the motive for most of the killings. Kuklinski would enter into a business deal with his intended victim. Once the victim would come up with the cash, Kuklinski would murder him. His weapon of choice was cyanide poison, which in many cases was hard to detect as the cause of death. He developed a method of injecting cyanide in an aerosol spray can. A spray in the face of his intended victim would effectuate the murder. In many cases, he would lace food with cyanide and give his victim his last meal. He also killed people by strangulation, shooting, and using a knife.

Detective Kane conducted an extensive toll analysis of Kuklinski's telephone, and there was a definite pattern. Det. Kane learned that whomever Kuklinski made telephone calls to over a period of time would turn up dead. The cause of death in many cases would be coronary arrest. Of course, cyanide hadn't been suspected and the cause of death was misdiagnosed. Detective Kane's superiors had not given him the investigative support that he needed, and he felt that it was time to conclude his investigation. They wanted Detective Kane's findings to be presented to the state grand jury even though the evidence collected at the time was not enough to try Kuklinski. Bob Carroll, the chief attorney in the Organized Crime Task Force, attended the meeting with the state police. When he returned to his office, he called me over and said, "Booch, wait until you hear about this case. We have to take it over. There is a guy from Bergen County who has probably killed a dozen or more business associates and probably was a hit man for Roy De-Maio, a Gambino Capo." We learned later that Bobby Carroll's victim estimate was a little short. It would probably be closer to one hundred victims. I never saw Bobby so excited about an investigation. He briefed me and I knew right from the start that we were going to be successful. Bobby not only was an excellent, hardworking prosecutor, but he also had a great investigative sense. I first met Bobby when he was an investigator with the Essex County Prosecutor's Office working his way through law school. We were a great team and had an excellent staff of investigators. I knew we could do the job. Of course we didn't want to insult the state police, so we decided that we should make it a team effort. We asked for Detective Kane to be assigned with us. After all, he deserved to stay involved as one of the lead detectives since it was his initiative and tenacity that brought the case thus far. Bobby Carroll and I brought our top investigators, Ron Donahue and Paul Smith, together for a strategy meeting. We felt the only way to get evidence would be from Kuklinski's own mouth. We needed someone who Kuklinski would trust enough to talk about his murders. Kuklinski worked alone, and anyone who had assisted him had already been murdered, so we had only one choice: an undercover police officer who could play the part of a mob hit man. We knew the best in the business—Dominick Polifrone, and Alcohol Tobacco and Firearms Agent. Dominick was a good friend and was a highly skilled undercover officer. Several years earlier he had successfully infiltrated the John Gotti crew in New York. Now all we had to do was talk Dominick into taking this assignment. We met with Dominick and after explaining our plan and describing Kuklinski; Dominick's first response was, "No way!" Then he asked, "Are you guys crazy? I love you guys, but there is no way I am going to do it. I'm in for a promotion, and this case could take over a year. Besides, I like my life, and if this guy ever suspects me, one spray into my Italian nose and you'll be saying what a good guy I was." He continued, "Besides, I don't want the state police backing me up; I would need street savvy detectives." The more Dominick made excuses, the more we knew he was going to do it. It was a challenge and we knew Dominick could not walk away from a challenge or a fight. He finally accepted, but with one condition. That Ron Donahue, Paul Smith, and me would always be his backup in case something went wrong. Now I tried to wiggle out of it. After all, I was the deputy chief and had a command I had to worry about. Of course, I loved it, and was going to stay as close to Dominick as possible. Nothing would happen to him on my watch. Dominick began his undercover assignment by frequenting one of Kuklinski's hangouts, a luncheonette in Paterson. We also initiated a wiretap on Kuklinski's home phone. Dominick was successful at meeting and befriending Kuklinski. And then one day it happened. Kuklinski admitted to murder, and it was on tape. We now wanted to lock it in. We came up with a scenario. Dominick had a Jewish kid from Livingston who had a lot of money and wanted to buy a large quantity of cocaine. Paul Smith would be the mark. Dominick arranged for the "Jewish kid" to bring the money to the Vince Lombardi Rest Area on the New Jersey Turnpike where they would take the money and Kuklinski would kill him. Our game plan was to arrest Kuklinski when he arrived at the rest area in a van, and in his possession would hopefully be either the cyanide spray or cyanide-laced sandwiches. I arranged for me, Paul, and Ron to meet at the rest area several hours before the scheduled Polifrone/Kuklinski meeting. Kuklinski never met the Jewish kid, so Paul Smith was cool. Ron would stay on the perimeter and Paul would stay in the restaurant. I would be the floater in and out of the restaurant. We would not talk to each other, in case there was counter surveillance. If we wanted to talk, we would give a signal and go into the men's room. I wore a yellow turtleneck and a black leather jacket and had my snub-nosed thirty-eight inside a rolled up newspaper so I'd be ready to react immediately if needed. When Dominick arrived, you wouldn't believe it, but he was also wearing a yellow turtleneck and black leather jacket. We kidded later about it. I said we looked like we were Pittsburgh Steelers. We had a state police teams unit at another location on standby for the arrest. It was my call when to make the arrest. Kuklinski was late. I gave Paul Smith the signal and we went into the men's room and stood by the urinals. The ugliest man I ever saw, clothes disheveled, matted, unkempt hair came in and stood by the urinal next to Paul Smith. Paul was youthful, clean cut, and good looking. This guy leaned toward Paul, looking down at Paul's penis, and started to moan. Paul looked at me with the funniest look I ever saw on his face, and let out a yipe. He looked at me and said, "This is above and beyond the call of duty" and bolted from the men's room. Later, I asked Paul why the weirdo approached him and if Paul had ever been a previous visitor to that men's room. Anyway, Kuklinski finally arrived but he didn't have the van. He and Dominick had a conversation in the parking lot. I wasn't going to let Dominick go anywhere with Kuklinski. If movement was made in that direction, I would have ordered his arrest. Dominick and I had prearranged signals, so I knew that there was just a delay and he had to go for the van. He was probably just doing a final test of Dominick. At one point, Kuklinski went to an outside phone booth to make a phone call. I took the booth next to his in an attempt to overhear his conversation, but I couldn't make out what he was saying. It was the first time I was actually able to see the size of the man. He was enormous and very scary. Dominick became my hero.

Kuklinski left the rest area and told Dominick that he would be back with the van. I had ordered a surveillance of Kuklinski's home in Demarest, and the state police reported that he had arrived home. We waited and waited and Kuklinski hadn't returned, so I ordered the state police teams to prepare to block the roads exiting his home and if Kuklinski departed, to make the arrest. Paul Smith and I proceeded to join with the state police by Kuklinski's house. Our surveillance team reported that Kuklinski was departing with his wife as a passenger and was heading directly toward us. I ordered the state police to create a roadblock and make the arrest. Paul and I were in the roadway behind the roadblock. When Kuklinski saw the roadblock, he drove off the roadway and around the roadblock directly at me and Paul. We pulled a John Wayne, Clint Eastwood type of act. We drew our weapons and pointed directly at the driver, Kuklinski. He slowed down, bent over as if to retrieve or place an object under his seat and hit the gas as if to go through us, but then came to a stop. Paul was to my right so he went to the driver's side and I went to the passenger's side. I opened the door with my left hand and held his wife against the back of the seat and out of harm's way. With my right hand, I pointed my gun at Kuklinski's head and told him not to resist. I then removed his wife from the car and several detectives behind me placed her in custody out of the way. She began screaming and Kuklinski started resisting but was overpowered. We hadn't hurt his wife, but he felt we were abusing her. We then found a loaded revolver under his seat and several cheese sandwiches, one of which was later determined to be laced with cyanide. Was that sandwich for the rich kid or Dominick? On January twenty fifth, nineteen ninety eight, Richard Kuklinski was convicted for three murders and was given two life sentences. He would be eligible for parole in sixty years. Anthony Bruno has written a book, *The Iceman,* and HBO has done several specials on his life. I have to credit Bobby Carroll for recognizing the importance of this case, Dominick Polifrone for his outstanding undercover work, and Det. Pat Kane, who never let go and for his excellent detective work on this case.

Chapter Thirty-two

Private Sector

In 1998 I decided to retire and try the private sector. After all, my task force had arrested and prosecuted over 500 made members of the Cosa Nostra. We had arrested and prosecuted Capo Anthony Acceturro, the Taccetta brothers, and associates and totally destroyed the New Jersey faction of the Lucchese crime family. The New Jersey faction of Philadelphia-based Bruno crime family no longer had any influence in New Jersey, with the arrests and convictions of the Bosses in Philadelphia and their inside war where they killed off most of their soldiers. The Gambino crime family, under the leadership of the notorious John Gotti, was wiped out with his conviction in New York and the prosecution and conviction of Robert "Cabert" Bisaccia and his crew in New Jersey. The conviction of DeCavalcante Boss John Riggi and the prosecution of practically his whole family ended this small but powerful New Jersey-based family. All of the Campisi family was prosecuted, and most are still incarcerated. The feds prosecuted the heads of the five families in New York that had an impact on what remained as the Bonanno and Colombo families' influence in New Jersey. My task force was instrumental in cleaning up the garbage, vending machine, construction, labor, and several unions, such as the Teamsters, Longshoreman, Hod carriers, Bartenders, and Operating Engineers, etc. The most important element that caused the decline of the Cosa Nostra in New Jersey was the breakdown of the code of omerta. The Cosa Nostra was no longer a secret organization. It seemed like everyone we arrested wanted to tell it all. There was total distrust among its members. I started by own company: "Corporate Integrity Consultant Company." I knew that there were many Italian-owned companies that wanted to clean their company of any association with organized crime. There were many companies that were under the scrutiny of law enforcement because of allegations that were either inferred or alleged. I felt that, because of my expertise, I could clean up these companies to the satisfaction of law enforcement. This turned out to be true. I started to make money as soon as I came out of the starting gate. I can't name the companies because of confidential clauses in our agreements, but the first month I had two $7,500-a-month contracts, three $5,000.00-a-month contacts, four $2,500-a- month contracts, and work I received from attorneys mounted to about $4000.00 a month. The money was good, but I missed locking up the bad guys. When I received a phone call from the newly appointed Union County Prosecutor Theodore Romankow, who asked me how I felt about being his chief of detectives, I simply asked, "When do I start?" It was the next day. I never asked for a contract or my salary. I just had to get back into law enforcement. I disbanded my company and went back to work in October 2002.

I found out immediately that my role was a lot different then what I was used to. In the prosecutor's office, the attorneys were in charge, and they made all the investigative decisions, not the detectives. My first week on the job I was told by one of the legal staff that I had to understand that, although I was part of the staff, I was still below all the assistant prosecutors and would have to comply with any order that even the youngest assistant prosecutor would give me. After I responded by saying, "Let me put it in terms that are easy for you to understand. If you or any attorney tries to order me around, I will grab him/her around their skinny neck and physically throw him/her out of my office." Well, I never heard from that individual again and I never had a problem.

Anyway, I had an excellent group of detectives and had the opportunity to bring on some talented detectives, and I was also able to promote some detectives who had been overlooked in the past. The office was primarily reactive not proactive. There were several outstanding detectives who were given a proactive function in my Narcotic Strike Force and my newly created Gang Task Force. I also initiated an Intelligence Unit that became recognized throughout the state as being a premier unit.

We did develop two, if you want to call them OC, investigations. One of them was a mix of some leftover members of the Lucchese and Gambino crime families. It wasn't a bad job, but it wasn't like the investigation we had in the past. To prove to you that the Cosa Nostra is not anywhere where it used to be, you won't believe this: The skipper of this crew was Andrew Knapik, who was not even an Italian. You got it. The Cosa Nostra no longer has any discipline or rules. However, there was another job, which I enjoyed immensely. Yes, the Gallicchio family all got out of prison, and guess what? They were in business again. One of the assistant prosecutors, Jim Tansey, initiated an investigation on the Gallicchio family. I have to say a few things about Jim Tansey. I have great respect for Jim, so here I go. Jim grew up in the Gallicchio neighborhood, the Vailsburg section of Newark, New Jersey. He not only had first-hand knowledge of the Gallicchios, but he himself had become addicted to drugs and alcohol. When he was a teenager, he bottomed out on drugs. He had no place to go. If he went down further with drugs, he would certainly die. So, with the strength of a supporting family, he picked himself up and cleaned up. He became a New York City Police officer and, although he had a recurring problem with drugs, he received an honorable discharge. He opened his own company and started making a lot of money. He went to law school and passed the New Jersey Bar. He lectured on alcohol and drug abuse and sponsored many abusers. The people he has helped are too many to acknowledge, but there are many who became very successful because of Jim's help. Jim Tansey knew the damage the Gallicchios brought to many families and the lives they had ruined, so once he received information that they were still in business, he had the Narcotic Strike Force target their operation. Under his and Captain Mike Bums' skilled leadership, an excellent investigation was conducted and once again the Gallicchio family was arrested and prosecuted. Hopefully this will be the last of Gallicchio family.

Law Enforcement no longer considered the Cosa Nostra a threat. When I look back at my career fighting the Cosa Nostra, I certainly feel that I had a lot to do with eliminating a cancer to our society. I am proud of my work and the work of many law enforcement officers who contributed to this effort. However, we may have significantly reduced the Cosa Nostra's influence in New Jersey, but while we were doing that, another cancer developed; one that is more dangerous than the Cosa Nostra, and that is the gang culture. Gangs have replaced the Cosa Nostra as the investigative priority by law enforcement. John Gatti, the infamous Boss of the Gambino crime family, when sentenced to life in prison, made a statement about the gangs' rise in power. He said, "Someday you (referring to law enforcement) will wish you had the Cosa Nostra back." Gotti recognized the seriousness of the gangs and the problems they were creating for law enforcement.

Chapter Thirty-three

Who are the Real Criminals?

I retired in 2000 and formed a LLC called Corporate Integrity Consultant Service. The service provided was cleaning up corporations that were accused of having an association with Organized Crime. I was doing extremely well but I found out that the Cosa Nostra was not the only entity that was criminal. The so-called legitimate professions were just as bad if not worse than the Cosa Nostra. Let me tell you how I came to realize that. Unfortunately, I have to change the names to protect the individuals not involved in any criminal conduct.

I was retained by two brothers who had a lucrative construction and commercial sheet rock company. They contacted me and I agreed to a consultant agreement of $7500.00 per month to rid their company of the stigma of organized crime. The brothers had to agree that they would do exactly what I told them to do, such as firing employees who had organized crime affiliation, discontinuing doing business with companies or persons associated with organized crime, and to respond truthfully to any interrogatories by me or the state.

The two brothers had a full ride to the University of Massachusetts and were star football players. In the summer they would do construction work in their father's small business. When they graduated, they bid on a large job at Harts Mountain and got the contract. The two brothers didn't have money to hire workers, so they worked day and night by themselves to satisfy that contract. They made a lot of money on that job and they start bidding on major jobs in New York. They grew up in Staten Island and were neighbors with many wise guys, including Sam "the Bull" Gravano. There is no doubt that they received the assistance of organized crime to get many of contracts they received. They had hired several wise guys and paid large salaries and did business with all organized crime companies. This was the only way to exist in New York during that time period.

The mistake they made was they applied for a license to bid on casino work, not knowing that the casino control commission did an extensive investigation to keep organized crime out of the casinos. When their investigation disclosed that the two brothers had organized crime ties, they not only denied the license but they contacted New York and it also hit the press. New York responded by canceling all their existing contracts in New York. This action would have killed their business.

They hired me to help rid their companies of any affiliation with organized crime, so I did my own investigation. Believe me, I uncovered more organized crime involvement then the detectives with the casino control commission. One thing I wanted to do was bring in an attorney who could be trusted. Several attorneys that they had were known by the state to represent Mafia individuals and companies. I did not need to be associated with mob attorneys. There was an attorney, Tom, who I knew for a long time. He was very successful and had an excellent reputation. I dealt with him numerous times when I was with the state. Of course, he was a phony at that time and simply used me by bragging to his clients that he had contacts in high places in law enforcement. He did the same thing to the FBI. He went to all their functions and became friends with every FBI supervisor who came to the Newark office. He would use that association to further his attorney business. Clients went to him believing that he could have the state police and the FBI assist his legal work for them. I also fell into that trap. I believed in his bullshit and talked the brothers into retaining him.

The first thing we had to deal with was the casino control commission's denial of their license. They had scheduled a hearing for us in Atlantic City. Our goal was to have the commission grant them a license, at which time I would have to prove that there was no organized crime involved in their construction companies. TD Paul Smith, my investigator, and I arrived and were waiting in the lobby when I was approached by a casino control commission's deputy attorney who apparently knew me, but I didn't recall ever meeting him. He was very cordial and he asked me straight out, "Bob, what is the story about these two brothers?"

I answered, "If you are asking me if there are any ties to organized crime, my answer is absolutely. There is a history of their association, especially with the Gambino family. But, let me tell you this. My job is to clean this company up and remove any and all associations with organized crime. I am doing that, and the day you see me no longer their consultant, you will know I failed. Right now I can say emphatically that I am being very successful."

When I was done speaking, the DAG said, "I know your reputation and believe you will be successful. I am prepared to give the brothers a license, but they have to agree that they will not bid on work for two years. Then, after two years, if you are still with their company, we will allow them to bid on work within the casinos." This was not only a home run but a grand slam. I immediately went in the lobby and told TD what just occurred. He asked me if I was stupid. "We can't make any money settling the matter." As we were speaking, the DAG came over and said he wanted to go on record with our agreement. TD responded and said, "I apologize, but I received an emergency call from home and have to leave." This was a down right lie. He didn't want to settle. He wanted to make as much money as he could. He stated, "This old junk yard dog is looking for a fight. I will win in court." I couldn't believe it, but it seemed I had to go along. After all, he was in charge. I never told the brothers.

TD told the brothers that he was going to fight the casino control commission and the New York attorney general's office in the courts and was confident he would win. He was given a million dollar retainer; I was pissed but still didn't say anything.

A couple weeks later, I ran into the chairman of the casino control commission, who I knew beforehand. In our conversation, he reiterated what I was told before. The Commission would grant the brothers a license, but they could not bid on a job for two years. If I was still with their company, they would they would be allowed to bid on work in Atlantic City. I again felt that this was a homerun. When I told TD, he went through the roof. He said I had no right to go behind his back and that what I did could be considered a crime. That evening he called for a meeting with the brothers. He stated, "Some stupid pepper went behind my back and approached the commissioner of the casino control commission. He was given a lot of bull and believes it. Well, this stupid guinea violated the law and has made it more difficult for me to defend these issues in court."

Well that was it for me. I stood up and said, "Who do you think you are, calling me a pepper and a guinea, and what law are you talking about. You are nothing but a shyster. I quit," and I walked out. The brothers followed me outside and asked me to return. I said, "How can you take what TD said. You are Italian and he works for you, but you didn't say anything." They responded by saying that they couldn't be thin skinned and that I should reconsider and not quit. That was it. It was obvious that the brothers accepted TD's bullshit, so I just left. Well, they stayed with TD as their attorney and eventually went bankrupt. TD went up to Albany to reinstate the brothers' licenses and lost in Court. TD made a lot of money and still was not able to get their casino licenses. One brother went to jail because of an association they had with a political figure. This never would have happened if I was still their consultant.

I again ask, "Who are the real criminals?" I wonder what your answer would be.

I FINALLY RETIRED

The time had come. I was seventy-six years old and, quite frankly, worn out. I had seen it all. I always considered that I was a good listener (an important quality for a chief to have). I caught myself not paying attention at meetings and detective briefings. It was time to leave law enforcement. November 1, 2013 was my last day. When I was cleaning out my office, all the memories of my career sped through my head. I still say to this day that I never had a bad day. That sounds ridiculous, but it's true. The days that at the time seemed bad when looking back were not that bad at all. Every bad day I either learned something positive or it helped groom me for a high position in law enforcement and contributed to my expertise. So those bad days turned out to be good days. While cleaning my office and boxing the many plaques, I started to cry. It was a sad time for me. I certainly believe that I reached my goal "to eradicate the Cosa Nostra in New Jersey." I could hardly think of a dozen mob guys that were still on the street. I felt that my job was done and wondered what the task force would be doing after I was gone.

Well, I packed up my personal car and left the parking lot still with tears in my eyes. As I drove through Elizabeth, I noticed that on every corner was a different gang. The Bloods, The Crips, the Latin Kings, etc. I realized that the Task Force would have its hands full. I am certain that there will be several young detectives who will fill my shoes.

Although I was not a fan of John Gotti, the Boss of the Gambino crime family, he made a statement while being brought to prison. "Someday, you (law enforcement) will wish you had the John Gotti's back." The end.

Statements Made to

Avoid Detection from the Police

1. "DONT TALK ON THIS PHONE. IT'S TAPPED" AND THEN THEY WHISPER THE REST OF THE CONVERSATION.

2. "ONE THING ABOUT ME, I NEVER TALK ON THE PHONE," AND GUESS WHAT, HE IS TALKING ON THE PHONE.

3. THE BOSS NEEDS A PACKAGE DELIVERED TO A SECRET APARTMENT. HE HAS AND WANTS ONE OF HIS SOLDIERS TO DELIVER IT, BUT CODES THE DIRECTIONS TO AVOID SURVEILLANCE BY THE POLICE. HERE IT GOES. "LISTEN TO ME AND DON'T FUCK UP. LEAVE YOUR HOUSE WITH THE PACKAGE. DRIVE A SHORT DISTANCE AND PULL OVER. LOOK IN YOUR MIRRORS AND SEE IF YOU ARE BEING FOLLOWED. IF YOU DON'T SEE A TAIL, START GOING AGAIN. DRIVE WEST ON ROUTE 80. THAT IS NOT THE WAY TO MY APARTMENT. AGAIN, SEE IF YOU ARE BEING FOLLOWED. IF YOU DON'T SEE A TAIL, MAKE A U TURN. SLOW DOWN TO ten MILES PER HOUR. NO TAIL, KEEP GOING. GET OFF AT THE PATERSON EXIT. WHEN YOU REACH BROADWAY, PARK THE CAR. GET OUT, AND TAKE A WALK. IF YOU DONT SEE ANYTHING SUSPICIOUS, GO BACK TO YOUR CAR. DRIVE TO BROAD STREET IN FRONT OF #423 BROAD STREET. THAT IS NOT WHERE MY

APARTMENT IS, BUT GO INSIDE AND GO UP AND DOWN THE ELEVATOR. NO ONE AROUND, LEAVE THE BUILDING. GO TO #430 BROAD STREET. GO UP AND DOWN THE ELEVATOR. DON'T SEE ANY TAIL, GO TO APARTMENT 4C, KNOCK ON THE DOOR. I WILL PEEK OUT. IF IT'S YOU I WILL OPEN THE DOOR.

NO ONE EVER SAID THEY HAD TO BE SMART TO BE IN THE MOB.

Court Testimony

My Tricks in Testifying

Crazy, but I liked testifying in Court. I was unorthodox. I totally forgot what we were taught in the academy. I did it my way. Here are some of the humorous court battles between me and defense attorneys.

Rule number one – I totally prepared myself before I testified. This was most important, because the defense attorney could not slip a fact by me. I would know in advance what the attorney was trying to accomplish.

My own style. I copied this from a Lodi old timer detective. I was in court watching his testimony. While on direct, he came across like he was stupid. He appeared to have trouble understanding the questions. When he finished his direct testimony, I am certain the defense attorney felt that he was going to have a field day with this detective. Boy, was he fooled. When the attorney asked a stupid question like, "How do you know my client committed a crime," the detective straightened his back, looked at the jury, and articulated all the reasons he knew. He had just waited for the opportunity when the attorney asked a stupid question and opened the door for his answer. I adapted that style and it always worked for me.

In the early '80s the state in presenting a case was not allowed to mention organized crime. When a police officer was assigned to an organized crime unit, he could not say it in court. The trial was in Ocean County and involved the bribery of an officer to dismiss charges against the Boss of the Genovese crime family's son .There were multiple defendants, all represented by high-priced attorneys. I did my routine when I gave direct testimony. A well-known attorney, Francis Hartman, was the lead attorney, and on his cross examination he was trying to compare my previous testimony with the police reports. Well, the word Genovese was in the report. He was finishing his cross of me and possibly assuming he had won, when he asked "Genovese, Genovese, what is this Genovese? I turned to the jury and gave an hour lecture on the Genovese crime family. I heard pencils breaking and there were several objections by the other attorneys. The even stipulated my expertise as an organized crime expert. The judge denied all their motions. Mr. Hartman opened the door and would simply look at me and asked if I was finished and for me to continue. Guilty, Guilty, Guilty.

I was on the stand during a hearing to qualify as an expert. The defense attorney was trying to present to the Court that I lacked the knowledge to become an expert. I hadn't any special training or had only read several books on the subject. Most if not all of my expertise came from my numerous investigations that I conducted. So I figured that when I returned to the stand I would read a list of my investigations, which should prove my expertise. There were objections because of the fact that the list was not provided to the attorneys in discovery. They won. Even without the list I was still qualified by the court. So, I figured I would have to counter that loss. I wrote on a piece of paper "Honey, bring home a pound of bologna and a loaf of bread and a dozen eggs." I put the paper in my top pocket and, while the defense attorney was questioning me, I would pull out the paper and look at it before I answered him. They went ballistic. There we go again! Buccino is reading from notes, totally against Your Honor's previous decision. The judge, in a stern voice, ordered me to turn over the note to him. When he read it, he handed it back and told me to tuck it away.

Al Marra was Bobby Cabert's attorney. He is an excellent attorney and goes all out when cross examining a witness. On cross with me he was screaming at me and he approached me and slammed documents in front of me. I calmly said, "Counselor, I don't mind your screaming or you approaching me with documents, but I strongly suggest you change your mouthwash". He backed up and said something stupid like "I should punch you in the mouth." I responded by asking him why he was backing up. He should come forward if he wanted to punch me. Anyway, it almost was a mistrial and I got my ass chewed out by the judge, but the jury was smiling at me, and that made it successful for me.

In Morris County Superior Court, the defendant was John DiGilio, who was accused of loansharking. I was to give expert testimony. DiGilio tried everything to keep me off the stand. He served me with a civil action and even offered me the police director's job in Bayonne. He stalled my testimony for days until finally Judge Smith ordered the testimony begin. When I started my testimony, DiGilio stood up and fell flat on his face. Looking at the jury but away from the judge, I counted him out with my fingers. The judge didn't know why the jury was laughing, but he gave me a look like he knew I had done something. DiGilio was found guilty.

Another rule I had was that if you answered yes to the last ten questions the defense attorney asked on cross examination, you got your ass kicked. When asked a question that required a yes or no answer, I would continue the answer by repeating my direct testimony. When stopped by the judge, it was my way of telling the prosecutor to ask me to continue my answer. When asked if I ever told a lie, I would answer "Counselor, I am a married man. Sometimes when I go out for a couple beers after work but tell my wife I was tied up at the office. I am telling white lies. So occasionally I tell white lies, but I never lie under oath." Again, the jury laughed and I won.

When asked "But isn't it possible," the attorney expects the witness to say, "Anything is possible." I would answer, "No. With what I know about the facts of this case, I do not believe that it's possible." Got you.

I WOULD GET INDICTED TODAY

The things I did were successful, but today I would go to jail. Like the time I was looking for someone who had an active warrant for his arrest. He had told people that I knew that I could never catch him because he was smarter than me. I went to three bookmakers looking for him. I didn't even knock. I just walked in on them. When they asked if I had a search warrant and I told them that is what I call my right shoe. Anyway, they didn't give much information, so I went to the townhouse where he was living with a girlfriend.

When I knocked, she came to the door. She was a very pretty blond and I asked her if her boyfriend was there. She answered "I don't have to answer you, but the answer is NO. Now get off my property."

I answered, "Since you're not the Blessed Virgin, I don't believe you, and so you are under arrest for hiding a fugitive." She immediately invited me into the townhouse to look for her boyfriend. He wasn't there. All his clothes were gone. I told her she was still under arrest, since I knew she knew his whereabouts. She gave it up. She said he was going to Vegas and was going to pick up a friend. But first he was going to his sister's to pick up some clothes. Sure enough, I went to his sister's home and peeked in the windows and there he was with suitcase in hand, ready to go. Got you. Was that procedure?

When I was a uniform trooper and stationed at Scotch Plains, one of our responsibilities was policing Warren Township, which did not have a police department. There was a sixteen= year-old kid who was constantly getting in trouble. One day, when school was just letting out, I decided to get a cup of coffee at a local luncheonette. It was also a place where the high school kids hung out and played the pinball machines. My mistake for going there. Anyway, I was at the counter drinking my coffee when there was a lot of laughter. When I turned to see what was going on, there he was. He had my state police hat on and was making supposedly funny gestures. I walked over to him and warned him never to touch my uniform. He clowned around and said, "Yes sir, Mr. Trooper." I went back to my seat and he took a seat right next to me. He said, "What a pretty uniform," and at the same time tried to touch my handcuff case. That was all I could take. I grabbed him by the back of his neck, pulled off his pants, and put him over my knee. I spanked the hell out of him. When he got off my knee with tears flowing down his cheeks, he bolted out of the luncheonette to the laughter of all his friends. Several weeks went by. When I would see him on the streets he was extremely polite and would address me as Mr. Buccino, sir. Then one day we received a call from the high school's vice principal, requesting a trooper. I responded. The VP had an after school discipline class and had left the room for a couple minutes. When he came back his set of keys was missing from the top of his desk. The keys were for every lock in the school. I looked in the room and guess what? My young man was in the class. I told the VP to have one student at a time come into the room for questioning. When the student would arrive I would simply ask, "Young man/ or young lady/ do you know where the keys are?" Of course they would not know. One at a time I would ask the same question and get the same denial until my young man came in to see me.

"YOU LITTLE SON OF A BITCH. WHERE ARE THE KEYS?"

"OUTSIDE BY THE BUSH" The VP almost fell off his chair. His toughest student gave it right up. I wonder why.

There was a motorcycle gang that was very intimidating. One night there were about fifteen of them in a Dairy Queen parking lot. Their leader, a fat guy with a full beard dressed in full leather, was there. I had a marked troop car and parked near the Dairy Queen exit. The leader kept pointing in my direction and they would all laugh. They were tempting me to do something foolish. I waited until they all left in single file with the leader following behind. I knew they were going to try something, and they did. They were on a narrow country road driving very slow. I was traveling behind the leader when he accelerated and did a wheely. He passed his comrades on the left and drove over lawns, with his group blocking me from passing them. At least they thought so. I accelerated and pursued him over the lawns. Nothing was going to stop me. I chased him for several miles. He lived in Watchung in a small house with a front open porch. He drove right to his home, dismounted, and ran to the porch. I drove right up the lawn, got out of the troop car, and chased him. I caught him as he climbed the stairs to the porch. I grabbed him by his beard and dragged him to my car while he was yelling "MOM, MOM, OUCH, MOMMY CALL THE POLICE, I'M BEING AT-TACKED!"

"Dummy, I am the police, and you are under arrest." I don't know. Was that excessive force?

Several members of the Campisi family were involved in a shooting on Route 3 in Clifton.

Another trooper and I were taking them to Newark and driving on Route 21 when Petey White said to me, "Buccino, you're from the old neighborhood." I answered "yes," and he said, "Yea, your mother used to give us blow jobs". I never roughed up or struck a prisoner. I just didn't believe in it. But, when a prisoner takes a personal shot at you like saying something nasty about your family, you cannot let them get away with it. I pulled the car over to the shoulder, got him outside the car, took off his handcuffs, and told him that if he could kick my ass I would let him go. I proceeded in kicking the shit out of him. When we got back in the car after about ten minutes of complete silence, he said in a sheepish voice, "Prn sorry." I would get indicted today.

Glossary

Mafia - Organized criminal network originating in Sicily.

Boss - Capo regime. The head of the Mafia family over all members/ Boss over 100 made men. Capodecimo - Boss over ten made men.

Famiglia - Family The entire criminal enterprise consisting of consigliere, capodecimo, soldiers, and associates. The head of this organization is the Boss.

Consigliere - The advisor to the Boss.

Capo - A captain in the Mafia.

Lieutenant - A rank in the Mafia that was created by law enforcement. It was used to define a member in Mafia who had great influence but was under a Capo but supervised a crew of sergeants and soldiers.

Soldier - A sworn member of the Mafia.

Associate - A non-member of the Mafia that was involved in the criminal conduct of the enterprise.

Cosa Nostra - This thing of ours. Synonymous with the American Mafia.
Wise guys - A member of the Cosa Nostra.

Good fellows - A member of the Cosa Nostra.

Crew - A gang of associates under the supervision of a soldier or capo.

Made man - A sworn member of the Cosa Nostra.

Loan-shark/Shylock - A person that lends money at usurious rates.

Hit – Homicide.

Omerta - Code of silence.

Commission - The Bosses of the seven families New York and New Jersey.

National Commission - Bosses of all the families in United States.

CPSIA information can be obtained
at www.ICGtesting.com
Printed in the USA
BVHW050903230323
661004BV00012B/297